STUDIES IN HISTORY, ECONOMICS AND PUBLIC LAW

EDITED BY THE FACULTY OF POLITICAL SCIENCE OF
COLUMBIA UNIVERSITY

Volume XIX] [Number 3

TRADE UNIONS AND THE LAW IN NEW YORK

A STUDY OF SOME LEGAL PHASES OF LABOR ORGANIZATIONS

BY

GEORGE GORHAM GROAT, Ph.D.

THE LAWBOOK EXCHANGE, LTD.
Clark, New Jersey
2003

ISBN 1-58477-309-X

Printed in the United States of America
On Acid-Free Paper

The Lawbook Exchange, Ltd.
33 Terminal Avenue
Clark, New Jersey 07066-1321

Please see our website
www.lawbookexchange.com
for a selection of our other publications and
fine facsimile reprints of classic works of legal history.

Library of Congress Cataloging-in-Publication Data

Groat, George Gorham, b. 1871
Trade Unions and the law in New York: a study of some legal phases of labor organizations / by George Gorham Groat.
p. cm.
Originally published: New York: Columbia University Press, 1905. (Studies in history, economics, and public law ; v. 19, no. 3).
Includes bibliographical references.
ISBN 1-58477-309-X (cloth: alk paper)
1. Labor unions—Law and legislation—New York (State) 2. Strikes and lockouts—Law and legislation—New York (State) I. Title. II. Studies in history, economics, and public law ; v. 19, no. 3.

KFN5560 .G76 2003
344.74701'88—dc2l 2002041291

STUDIES IN HISTORY, ECONOMICS AND PUBLIC LAW

EDITED BY THE FACULTY OF POLITICAL SCIENCE OF
COLUMBIA UNIVERSITY

Volume XIX] [Number 3

TRADE UNIONS AND THE LAW IN NEW YORK

A STUDY OF SOME LEGAL PHASES OF LABOR ORGANIZATIONS

BY

GEORGE GORHAM GROAT, Ph.D.

New York
THE COLUMBIA UNIVERSITY PRESS
THE MACMILLAN COMPANY, AGENTS
LONDON: P. S. KING & SON
1905

PREFACE

THE following pages form part of a study of labor organizations—a study which the writer expects to complete in the near future. The completed work will embrace an examination of trade unions viewed as a factor in the economic activity of New York state.

The portion here presented includes two parts. The first deals with efforts to secure legislation favorable to the interests of organized labor. It aims to describe the more important legislative activities of the state federation. The second part deals with the lawfulness of trade-union activities. It traces the development of the law and of those decisions of the courts that pertain to the legal status of labor unions.

The effort throughout has been to determine the controlling principles, economic or social, and to ascertain, as far as possible, to what extent these principles conform to the wider economic and social principles upon which the present industrial life depends.

In the parts of the work not yet ready for publication the non-legal phases will be taken up, and attention will be devoted to the practical activities of trade unions in their efforts to influence to their advantage economic activity.

The sources referred to are only such as furnish material at first hand, as the proceedings of the annual conventions of the State Workingmen's Assembly and of the State Workingmen's Federation; the constitutions of these organizations; the session laws of the state; the reports of the decisions of the courts; and the annual reports and the quarterly bulletins of the state department of labor. For convenience a table is appended stating the cases to which reference is made, and, furthermore, stating the time at which each decision was made and by what court. Much valuable information has also been secured through interviews with labor leaders and with others who are conversant with the practical side of the movement.

Finally, the writer takes this opportunity to acknowledge his debt of gratitude to the members of the faculty in Economics in the School of Political Science. The helpful suggestions, the kindly advice, and above all the guiding inspiration of these men have done much to enable the author to accomplish what is here presented.

G. G. G.

NEW YORK, *May*, 1905.

CONTENTS

PAGE

CHAPTER VI.

CHAPTER VII.

CHAPTER VIII.

CHAPTER IX.

CHAPTER X.

CHAPTER XI.

TABLE OF CASES

CHAPTER I

NUMERICAL STRENGTH

In any attempt to estimate the influence of organized labor in this state, the numerical strength is a consideration of first importance. While it is undoubtedly true that the number of organizations and the number of members fail to give a wholly accurate idea of the influence exerted by them, yet the numbers must necessarily set forth an idea of the possibilities as no other facts could do. This is true for two reasons. Not all the local unions are affiliated with the state organization, and hence the entire strength of the movement is not concentrated. The importance of this consideration should not, however, be exaggerated. When awakened to some common interest there is a bond that draws them together even though they are unaffiliated. In such a case the numerical strength becomes important. In the second place, much depends on the individual ability of leaders, a force that cannot be estimated numerically. In case a leader shows unusual ability he will become much more formidable when the united membership is behind him. Especially is this true when the contest is of a political nature.

The following table gives figures to show the growth in numerical strength during the past eleven years. It is compiled from the reports issued by the state department of labor. The fact that the figures for the same year vary somewhat in the different annual reports shows that they are not exactly accurate.[1] The variations are, however, so slight as to be safely negligible. As to the accuracy of the reports issued by the department, it can only be said that they are as nearly accurate as the conditions make it possible to have them. The very loose and inadequate manner in which the unions themselves keep their records, and the frequent desire on their part to sacrifice fact for effect, make it extremely difficult to present any statement of numerical strength with more than approximate exactness. The table is offered with the feeling that it does give a fairly adequate idea of what has been accomplished during the period:

Year	Number of Organizations	Gain During the Year	Total Membership	Men	Women	Gain During the Year
1894[2]...	860	......	157,197	149,709	7,488	—
1895[2]...	927	67	180,231	170,129	10,102	23,034
1896[3]...	962	35	170,296	....	....	9,935[4]
1897[5]...	1,009	47	168,454	162,690	5,764	1,842[4]
1898....	1,087	78	171,067	163,562	7,505	2,613
1899....	1,320	233	209,020	200,932	8,088	37,953
1900....	1,635	315	245,381	233,553	11,828	36,361
1901....	1,871[6]	236	276,141	261,523	14,618	30,760
1902....	2,229	358	329,098	313,589	15,509	52,957
1903....	2,583	354	395,598	380,845	14,753	66,500
1904....	2,505	78[4]	391,681	378,864	12,817	3,917[4]

The figures in the table show the net increase from year to year. Yet they convey no adequate idea of the

[1] In every case the last figures stated have been the ones inserted in the table.

[2] June 30. [3] October 31. [4] Decrease.
[5] From 1897 to end—September 30. [6] Given in some tables as 1,881.

variation from month to month. This variation appears not only in the disbanding of organizations and the appearance of new ones to take their places, but also in the changes of membership which are continually occurring within the organizations. When we look at these unions as a factor in the economic and social life of the state, the permanency of the organizations and the steadiness of membership are important considerations. It is true that the main portion—by far the larger portion—of the membership is permanent, and that portion which is united into the state federation is as permanent and as substantial as any of the factors in industrial life. The table shows, then, the net results—the net gain after all the variations have been balanced.

A few cases taken at random will serve to show how extensive are the variations. During the first six months of 1904, 143 new unions were formed. In the same period 170 unions either disbanded or amalgamated. This left a net decrease of 27 unions. During the year from April, 1902, to April, 1903, 435 new organizations appeared. Of these 299 were formed during the first six months, and 136 during the remainder of the period. The first period included the warmer months of the year, and showed the larger gain. The six months' period immediately following shows 216 as the total number of new unions. During that period 62 were disbanded and 18 were amalgamated, leaving a net gain of 136. In 1902 the period from April to October shows 390 new organizations with a loss of 91, leaving a net gain of 299. One town showed 72 unions in March, 1903, 80 in September of the same year, and 68 in March of the following year. These instances will serve to illustrate the continual variations among the unions.

As to the size of the unions, the following is indicative:

In 1900 there were 15 unions having each a membership of less than five; 32 unions having each a membership of over 1,000. The average membership of the 1,635 unions in that year was 150. One-fourth of the entire membership was in unions having each a membership of 1,000 or more; nearly another one-fourth (24 per cent) in unions with a membership of from 201 to 500. Fifteen per cent of the unions had a membership of between 501 and 1,000; seventeen per cent had a membership of between 101 and 200. Eighty-two per cent of the entire membership was in unions with over 100 members.

While the number of unions is varying continually, there are also striking cases of variation in membership. A wave of unionism may strike a place, and the growth will be phenomenal. An entire town may be unionized in a few weeks, and then a gradual reaction will set in until a normal condition is reached. This fact will account for some of the most striking increases in membership. Yet it is not to be inferred that it is the only cause. Industrial conditions have an important influence; the personal efficiency of the organizer has its effect; also the season of the year, for the summer months seem in many cases more favorable for increase of membership than the winter months. In the summer of 1902 membership was increased in Schenectady from 2,786 to 8,856. In September, 1903, it reached 10,168. During the following six months it fell to 8,032. The losses of membership in the state in several trades were heavy during the winter of 1903–4. The clothing and textile trades lost 2,158; the metals, machinery, *etc.*, trades, 6,804; the wood-working trades, 1,042; the miscellaneous trades, 4,162. This loss was counteracted in large part by a gain in the building industry of 11,754, mainly due to the addition of a large union of Italian laborers in

New York City. During the same period the transportation trades made the relatively large gain of 5,678. The theatrical trades gained 800. There was a decline of 600 in the number of women. Such are some of the changes continually occurring in membership of which a statement of net results gives a very inadequate idea.

As a general rule, the larger cities show the widest variations in membership and the smaller ones in the number of organizations. Of the 30,907 gain in membership between April and October, 1903, all but 8,000 was gained in seven large cities of the state. These same cities furnished only 97 of the 225 gain in organizations. In New York City there was a total gain of 45 unions, with a loss of 17, leaving a net gain of 28, while during the same period there was in the entire state, except New York City, a total gain of 107 organizations, with a loss of 76, leaving a net gain of 31. In another year New York City gained 64 new organizations and 24,000 members, while the rest of the state gained 294 organizations and 29,000 members. Of 77,000 new members in 1903, 35,000 were added in New York City and 42,000 elsewhere. In another six months New York City added 18,000 compared with 10,000 elsewhere. In yet another period the city made a distinct gain while the rest of the state lost nearly 3,000. From these typical instances it will appear how large at times is the variation in membership.

CHAPTER II

DEVELOPMENT OF STATE FEDERATION

THE effort on the part of labor in New York state to influence legislation has been above all an organized effort. The degree of perfection of such organization being dismissed from consideration until a later chapter, the fact of organization remains. The oldest and most distinctively state organization was the Workingmen's Assembly. The history of its inception was briefly outlined in the address by the president of that association in 1891. It may be summed up as follows: In 1864 a bill was introduced in the legislature known as the Hastings' Strike Bill. In those days the various labor unions of the state were forming and strengthening their local organizations necessarily with a considerable degree of secrecy, because of the restrictive laws then in force. The bill, though considered "a direct stab at labor, struggling at that time for protection," appears not to have been extreme. In the course of debate Senator Folger offered amendments still more unfavorable to labor. Hastings withdrew his support entirely when the amendments were offered, and the measure became known to its opponents as "Folger's Anti-Trades Union Strike Bill." The Plasterers' Union and Typographical Union No. 6, both of New York City, led the way in passing resolutions of protest, and similar resolutions came from other trade unions of the state. A large mass-meeting was held at Tompkins Square, New York

City, at which the measure was hotly denounced and Senator Folger burned in effigy. The bill was killed. The unions saw in the death of the bill a direct result of their unity of action. There now arose among them a feeling of the necessity for organization in order to secure protection "in relation to legislation as well as the question of wages and hours of labor." "From that victory in 1864," concludes the president, "the seeds of a great and grand organization were sown." In 1865 the Workingmen's Assembly was organized. The defensive was soon laid aside for the aggressive and earnest agitation was begun. In 1871 the problem of prison labor was taken up and a commission secured to investigate existing conditions. An apprenticeship law was passed in the same year. From these beginnings the organization entered upon the advocacy of one measure after another until the movement came to assume the high degree of complexity that now characterizes it.

The Workingmen's Assembly continued as a separate organization until 1897. In the meantime two other state organizations had grown up. One was a state branch of the American Federation of Labor organized in 1881, and the other the district assemblies of the Knights of Labor organized in 1869. These were formed in the state as a part of the normal growth of the national organizations. The Workingmen's Assembly, though formed before any of the national organizations, does not seem to have exercised any direct influence on the formation of either of the other two. They appear to have been the result rather of a separate movement on the part of the various central labor unions of cities, not all within the state. In 1897 the Workingmen's Assembly united with the New York state branch of the American Federation of Labor, under the name of the "Workingmen's Federation of the State of New York." This amalgamation was accomplished after about seven years of discussion enforced by the experience of rivalry and clashing interests detrimental to substantial progress. For a few years after this efforts were made to unite the new organization with the Knights of Labor. It seemed for a time as if this union might be accomplished. More recently, however, the two organizations have found that they are growing farther apart, and it is scarcely probable that any amalgamation will be effected in the very near future.

The constitution of the older organization varied but little and only in minor points from that of the new organization. The constitution of the Workingmen's Assembly, as it stood in 1884, is practically the constitution of the Workingmen's Federation, as it stands today. The organization consists of "such trades unions and labor organizations as shall conform to its rules and regulations." Its objects are two in number:

> To agitate such questions as may be for the benefit of the working classes, in order that we may obtain the enactment of such measures by the state legislature as will be beneficial to us, and the repeal of all oppressive laws which now exist. To use all means consistent with honor and integrity to so correct the abuses under which the working classes are laboring as to insure to them their just rights and privileges. To use our utmost endeavors to impress upon the various divisions of workingmen the necessity of a close and thorough organization, and of forming themselves into local unions wherever practicable.[1]

Thus the two objects of state organization, as embodied

[1] This was the same in the Workingmen's Assembly constitution in 1869. It is in the present constitution—Article ii, secs. 1, 2.

in the constitution, are to obtain beneficial legislation and to secure more thorough organization. In 1889 a clause was added providing that "no business shall be transacted but that which is of a legislative nature, in the interests of labor." This attempt to restrict the field of action of the Assembly proved unsatisfactory to the newly formed organization in 1897, and in the new constitution the clause does not appear. This was undoubtedly due to the difference in attitude of the two consolidated organizations. The Assembly, as the clause states, confined its attention entirely to legislative work. The branch of the American Federation maintained a much more intimate relation to the unions whose delegates constituted its conventions and sought often to regulate their affairs. In the amalgamation the ideas of the Federation have survived. The following standing committees, provided for by the constitution, show the scope of the work of the conventions. They are the committees on (1) president's address, (2) finance, (3) resolutions, (4) grievances, (5) general good of organization, (6) constitution, (7) labels. Other special committees are appointed at each session as occasion requires.

It is provided by the constitution, in fixing the conditions of membership in the annual convention, that "no person holding a political appointment shall be eligible as a delegate, unless working at his trade or calling;" "no person shall be eligible . . . who publicly advocates the election of any candidate for political office who has been placed on the unfair list;" "any person holding a political appointment representing organized labor shall be entitled to a seat in the convention without voice or vote."[1] The second of these provisions is more recent than either

[1] Constitution, art. iii, secs. 8, 9.

of the other two. Until 1888 delegates after their term had expired were entitled to seats without voice or vote.[1]

Since 1883, at least, the provision of the following section has been in force:

> A legislative committee shall be elected at each annual session . . . to be composed of three delegates. This committee shall have power to supervise all legislation originating in this Workingmen's Assembly [later the Federation] and shall have power to alter or change any bills, provided that the spirit and intent of such measures shall be preserved.

Further, the chairman is required to "be present during the session of the legislature," and to "attend to the entire business himself," for which service remuneration was provided. The organization of this committee has been subject to several changes. At first the three members were chosen one each from Albany, Troy and Cohoes, and were to receive "such compensation as shall remunerate them for lost time." In 1885 the residence requirements were "Albany, Troy and vicinity." The designation of places has since been dropped. In 1888 one member elected by the committee was to be present at least forty days of the session, for which a fixed sum per diem was to be paid. The following year "the person so elected" was to attend "to the entire business himself," except when he should deem it necessary to call the members of the committee together for consultation. The payments for such legislative service were to be made weekly. In 1892 weekly payments were abolished. In addition to the legislative committee, the Workingmen's Assembly had an executive council whose duties were to review the reports made by the legislative

[1] This provision for seating ex-delegates was in the constitution of 1869.

committee; "to issue the records of the members of the senate and assembly . . . on all measures emanating from this body;" and to assist the president and the committee when called upon to do so. In the new constitution the legislative committee was charged with the duty not only "to make a complete report on all measures," but also to present a "tabulated record of members of the senate and assembly on the same." Thus these two committees were placed in charge of important duties, and they became very prominent factors in the effort to shape legislation. This is shown more at length in the following chapter.

CHAPTER III

THE STATE FEDERATION AT WORK

THE present chapter attempts to throw some light on the practical influence exerted by organized labor on the course of legislation. Many labor organizations have existed for a time or for a particular purpose no record of whose proceedings has been preserved. Yet the general similarity between all such organizations makes the problem less difficult than it would otherwise be. The major portion of the material upon which this chapter is based is taken from the proceedings of one or two organizations,[1] for the reason that their records were the only ones available. At the same time, they have been used in the confidence that, although only partially representing organized labor as a whole, they nevertheless give a fairly satisfactory picture of the general influence that is being exerted for the purpose of securing the passage of laws.[2]

The consideration of legislative methods may be conveniently divided into three parts: (1) the workings of the annual conventions in session, including preliminary

[1] The Workingmen's Assembly and the Workingmen's Federation.

[2] It is a matter of regret to the student of these problems that the larger libraries of the state have neglected to collect and preserve copies of the proceedings of labor conventions as well as other material pertaining to the labor movement. Such material must inevitably increase in value as trade unions continue to grow in economic and political importance.

work; (2) the efforts to seat or unseat senators and assemblymen according to their "records;" (3) the work done during the session of the legislature, mainly by the legislative committee.

The conventions, which are held every year (usually during the month of September), are held at a time which has been chosen with some care. In this matter experience seems to have led them to conclusions different from those reached by the national organization. The convention of the latter is held as soon as the President's message is in and before Congress settles down to serious work. This gives them the space in the public press which has just been filled by the presidential message, and enables them to consider its recommendations and to formulate their measures for Congress in time for its deliberation. In New York state the conventions were until recently held in January immediately after the opening of the state legislature. The time of meeting was changed, however, so as to enable the committee to complete its work and to get it before the legislature as early as possible. The January convention did not give sufficient time for this. Another important reason for changing the time was in order that the work of the convention might be made known to candidates before election. This would enable them to influence the choice of legislators as well as to control their votes after their election.

The convention itself initiates many measures. It also acts in many cases as a revising, adjusting and regulating body. It is made up of delegates, one, two or three in number, from such trade unions and labor organizations as belong to the Federation; the number of delegates being determined by the membership of the respective local unions. Central unions are entitled to one delegate each. Measures for legislative consideration may originate in any of these unions, local or central, and may be either recommended for legislation by a resolution or presented to the convention in the form of a drafted bill. Before being brought upon the floor of the convention, each resolution or drafted bill is considered by the executive council. An endorsement by this body will greatly strengthen the measure when before the convention, but the disapproval of the council does not prevent its being introduced independently. In the same way a measure originating with a local union may be endorsed by the central union of which that local is a member and that endorsement will have influence; but the withholding of that endorsement does not prevent the introduction of the measure before the convention. In practice, any local union which has a measure to urge will seek first the endorsement of its central union and then that of the executive council. A large number of the questions come before the convention in this way and the approval of the central bodies or of the executive council usually insures for the measure a favorable consideration, if not a favorable vote. The large central bodies are more active in originating bills than are the smaller ones, while comparatively few measures are initiated by local unions not united in centrals. Thus the articulation of local unions, central bodies and state organizations has been growing more perfect as the needs for co-operation and unity of effort have developed.

But with such a stream of bills and resolutions coming from such a variety of sources and representing such a complexity of interests often conflicting in character, the work of adjustment is indeed no easy matter, and the sessions of the convention are often exciting. In general the work of the convention is outlined by the executive council in the form of a program or list of measures. Copies of such programs are previously sent to each of the unions for their consideration before the time of the convention, and delegates often come instructed by their unions on particular measures. At present the proceedings of the convention are made as public as possible, though this has not always been the practice. The convention during its session listens to the report of the president outlining the general situation and calling attention to such particular questions as may be of current importance. The report of the legislative committee is also presented, describing the work of the past session of the legislature, recounting the fate of bills and the attitude of members of committees, and making special recommendations. The convention is divided into the seven standing committees provided for by the constitution, and such other additional committees as may be necessary. To these committees all matters are referred for consideration. This regulation applies to all measures, both those previously instituted by local unions and those inaugurated by the convention itself. An important rule is that each committee must report, either favorably or unfavorably, on every bill or resolution referred to it. Their reports are then either adopted or rejected by the convention. A large number of the resolutions fail of a favorable report from the committee. The number varies, and different estimates are made. One reliable authority fixes it at about thirty per cent. The general policy of the conventions is stated by one intimately connected with their workings to be "to take favorable action for legislation upon propositions concerning which there is entire agreement, and to avoid that on which there is division."

No matter how many conflicting interests may appear

in the convention, after the adjournment there stands a definite program for the coming session of the legislature. This program is placed in charge of the legislative committee. This committee supervises the bills of the Federation after the convention has adjourned, having power to alter them at will to meet any special emergencies that may arise, provided that "the spirit and intent of such measures shall be preserved."

Thus it appears that the purpose of the organization is accomplished up to this stage in a very thorough manner. Out of the extreme complexity in the beginning has come in the end a well defined policy as the result of a well organized system of selecting, rejecting and uniting.

The bills of the Federation must now, if possible, be enacted into law. For this purpose efforts to influence members of the legislature already seated are not sufficient. If members can be nominated and elected who are in favor of labor in general, much is gained at the beginning. There are, in general, two ways of working to secure such results. One is by independent local action to nominate a candidate within a district, and, if possible, elect him. The other is to unite the voting force within a district and to turn it in favor of that party candidate already nominated who will make the best pledges. From preference the unions seem to choose the former, but conditions often give them the balance of power where they have not strength enough to carry an independent nomination. Hence they more frequently accept the pledges, relying as best they may upon their redemption.

In 1884 a circular was sent out to the local unions of the Workingmen's Assembly advising them "to organize for the purpose of electing labor representatives to the legislature." Candidates at this time were nominated for the assembly by the workingmen in "a number of districts of the state." Two of these nominees were elected, one in Troy and one in Utica, and a nominee in Albany failed by only fourteen votes.[1] The lesson which the officials of the organization drew from this as stated in their report was that "these results show the power of the workingmen if they would but combine politically on legislative candidates." That but two members were so elected at the time might be taken as showing equally well the weakness of the efforts on the part of the workingmen to combine. This view is greatly strengthened by the fact that the plan has not grown to larger proportions. In 1892 a resolution was adopted directing the executive committee to select two assembly districts in the state having a large labor vote and to request the political party having control of these districts to nominate a qualified member in good standing in any labor organization in harmony with the Workingmen's Assembly who should voice the sentiments of labor on the floor of the assembly. This resolution indicates a general change in practical policy, a change which has grown out of the fact that however enthusiastic a laboring man may be in the interests of labor, he is at the same time something more than a laborer, and that this something holds him by ties too strong to permit of independent local political action. Together with this tendency came a practical objection which evidently was not at first foreseen. There were men of influence in the legislature who had served well the interests of labor. These men noticed the nomination of independent labor candidates. They made it known in unmistakable terms

[1] *Proceedings of the Workingmen's Assembly*, 1884.

that they saw no point in continuing to advocate labor measures only to have labor candidates nominated against them at the next election. They might have added further that for the same reason they would be unable to secure support from any of their colleagues in the future. The present tendency is away from independent nominations, at least until they can be made more general than district nominations, and towards the use of organized balance of power, in order to turn the scale as far as possible in favor of one of the candidates already nominated. The latter policy figured largely as a reason for the decision to change the time of meeting of the annual convention. A January convention formed a program too late to influence nomination and election. A September convention would enable the work of the executive council to be completed in time for use in a campaign. Reasons are still urged in favor of holding the conventions in August, on the ground that "if a convention were held in August you could list the bills adopted. . . . . offer them to prospective candidates for office, secure their promise of support, and failing of that, use your ballot on election day for those who will."[1] Every effort is now made by leaders of the labor movement to seat friends of labor from both parties and then rely on their assistance for the passage of bills. In these efforts they are supported in a greatly varying degree by the labor voter. In general, he is prevented by numerous other considerations from following blindly the candidate who is most outspoken in his loyalty to the cause of labor.

One way of getting a candidate to commit himself is to submit to him in public a pledge. These pledges are drawn up by the executive council and sent out to every

[1] This probably has reference to primaries.

senate and assembly district. In various ways and with as great publicity as possible the leaders in these districts ask the candidates to pledge themselves. The pledges name the leading measures to be presented at the coming session. This is well illustrated by the following, chosen at random from the reports:

The committee decided to present the following pledges to all candidates for senator and member of assembly: Weekly Pay Bill; Establishing a Bureau of State Printing; To abolish all Contracts on State Work; Uniform Text Books; Equalization of Taxes.

The number of measures inserted varies from year to year, but the intention is to include the few bills which are regarded as of greatest importance.

It is difficult to show the actual result of a system of pledging. It has been in practice for several years and no evidence of its discontinuance appears. Yet it has been modified and resolutions have been offered favoring its entire abandonment. A good authority states that it accomplishes nothing at all. It is, however, the only centralized effort that is made. All other efforts depend much upon the locality, and vary greatly in efficiency according to the degree of enthusiasm that exists locally for the labor movement.

The confidence of the leaders themselves in these methods appears in the following extracts from the proceedings: "Members of labor organizations have been elected to municipal and state legislative bodies, a rather tardy but happy awarding to the efficiency of the ballot when used with discretion." Speaking of the same subject, the president said in 1884:

That the workingmen can give the control of the legislature

to either party was clearly demonstrated last fall. The last legislature was Democratic in both branches, and was made so by the promise to abolish contract convict labor in the prisons. The party violated that promise and in punishment for these false pledges the workingmen, through the ballot box, have given both branches to the Republicans. Such lessons will teach political parties to faithfully carry out their pledges to labor or suffer defeat.[1]

In this way a program of labor bills is prepared for presentation, and efforts are made to secure legislators who will favor them. The problem that now confronts the managers may be summed up as follows: Given a number of bills to be enacted into law and a legislature only a few of whose members can be relied upon as friends through thick and thin, how can the greatest possible number of these bills be passed with the fewest possible changes?

The organization's chief reliance for the accomplishment of this end is the legislative committee. The central figure of this committee is its chairman. The chairman is assisted directly by the other two members of the committee. The committee is aided materially by the executive council, which consists of the president, seven vice-presidents and the secretary-treasurer. These committees represent the strength of the state organization, and the state organization is backed by the central and local trade unions and labor organizations within the Federation. By the provisions of the constitution

the chairman of the legislative committee shall furnish to the president of the Federation a weekly report of the proceedings of the legislature in relation to labor bills that have been endorsed by this body, the president to send a copy of such re-

[1] *W. A. Proceedings* (1884).

port to each central labor body and labor paper of the state. He shall make a complete report on all measures emanating from this body [the Federation], in his charge during the session of the legislature to the convention, with a tabulated record of the members of the senate and assembly on the same.[1]

This arrangement both centralizes very effectively the influence of the organization, and keeps the central figure in very close communication with all the local unions.

To describe definitely and accurately the work of this committee is difficult owing to the scope of its powers, the variety of their use and the complexity of the interests involved. As has previously been pointed out, it is impossible to estimate mathematically the results. The only way to secure an adequate idea of the extreme patience, tact and watchfulness necessary to accomplish any results at all is to follow the work of a committee through a session of the legislature. A fairly clear idea may be gained from a reading of the reports of the committee and the resolutions and discussions of the annual conventions. The core of the work consists in taking the bills, getting them introduced, attending the hearings before committees, and urging individuals to vote favorably when the matter comes to a vote before the house. Yet if this were all that the committee did, no results at all could be expected. When is a bill to be introduced? Shall it be introduced in the assembly first, the senate first, or simultaneously in both? This settled, which assemblyman or which senator shall be chosen to introduce it? Will the bill be given a hearing? Who should be secured to advocate the bill at the hearing? Will the bill ever be reported from the committee? If so, will it be amended? Will

[1] Constitution of the Workingmen's Federation, art. v, sec. 5.

it come to a final vote? If the bill lives through all this, there are the same dangers awaiting it in the next house, and in addition arise the questions: Has it passed the first house in time? If amended, is there time for a reconsideration? If finally passed, will it be signed or vetoed? Multiply these dangers by the number of bills to be cared for, and the product gives only a part of the duties and responsibilities of a chairman of the legislative committee. The reports show that more bills are introduced in the assembly than in the senate, and proportionately more bills pass the assembly than pass the senate. In 1888 there were thirteen bills to be introduced. The legislative committee secured a conference with the assembly members "who were known to be affiliated with organized labor," recognizing that "it was very essential that the members of the legislature in our favor should co-operate with us." Seven members responded, and the thirteen bills were divided among them for introduction. The work of the legislative committee at the time of committee hearings is of extreme importance, and at this point failure awaits by far the larger number of bills. Even while the measures are before the governor, the committee is still at work, and a conference between the governor and the chairman and president of the Federation is by no means unusual.

The duties already described make the work of the committee extremely complicated. But other matters increase the complexity. There was for a time no labor committee in the legislature, and labor bills were distributed among the various other committees for hearing. This often resulted in several hearings being set for the same hour, as well as in increasing the number of committees to be watched. As a result of persistent efforts a labor committee was secured, and matters were to that extent simplified. There has been scarcely a single report made by a committee to a convention in which the warning has not been given, "We have too many bills." "The greater the number of bills urged the less our chances on any of them." "This convention attempts to handle too many bills, and we believe that if determined action was taken, and only two or three bills presented at each session, more work would be accomplished." A drawback "which has existed for several years, and which is becoming more prevalent every year, is the large number of bills turned over to the committee to be forced through the legislature."[1] "The number of bills increases largely" was again the complaint as late as 1899. Not only is the number of bills a detriment, but many of them prove to be poorly drafted, and much time is lost in correcting them, if indeed they are not thrown out entirely because of this fault. In 1890 the president called attention to this in his annual address: "I would further recommend that all bills that we pass for the legislature be examined with care and all defects removed therefrom, so that the legislative committee will be enabled to present an almost perfect bill." "Sometimes," reports the committee, "bills come into the hands of your committee in such bad shape that it is necessary to have a lawyer revise them."[2]

In addition to these drawbacks, other obstacles to the easy passage of labor measures arise. Previous to 1897 there were each year three separate legislative committees urging three separate programs. These programs resembled each other in only a few leading features and

[1] *Workingmen's Assembly Proceedings*, 1886, 1889.

[2] Lawyers are not allowed as delegates in the conventions.

differed in numerous essential points.[1] With the organization of the Federation two of the committees were consolidated, leaving two still in the field. These two now present to the legislature two separate programs and there appears to be at times considerable rivalry between them. It not infrequently happens that two labor bills on the same subject will be introduced, one from each committee. This will often necessitate delay before the committee of the legislature while the two legislative committees confer and adjust the matter in some form of compromise draft which both can advocate. Separate local unions, after failing to get a measure of their own placed on the program of bills, often introduce it themselves through their local representative. It is then urged as a labor bill, though perhaps for some good reason opposed by one or both of the legislative committees. This has at times led to great confusion and much uncertainty as to what are labor bills and what are not. The report of 1892 states that the experience of that year had in it a lesson. Though the lesson has not been fully learned, extracts from the report will illustrate the conditions referred to.

There is no previous record of so large a number of bills being introduced or so many representatives of labor organizations being present. The Workingmen's Assembly, the state branch of the American Federation of Labor and the Knights of Labor, also several small societies, each had a full committee present. There was a deluge of labor bills. Not one real labor bill became a law. Members of the legislature who have watched and been friendly to labor legislation for years say there was too much of it, and they were right. To say that fifty labor measures were introduced is putting it mildly.

[1] In 1893, for example, over 40 so-called labor bills were presented.

During the agitation against the Pinkerton men three separate bills were urged by the three organizations at one time, in 1891, and each committee worked hard to get its own bill reported in preference to either of the others. Finally the codes committee, to which the measures had been referred, told the contending parties that if they would draft a bill agreeable to all concerned such a bill would be reported favorably. The president, in referring to the disadvantages of not always working together, said: "Such diversity tends in a great measure to weaken our efforts, to defeat our plans and to prevent us from securing the legislation necessary for our protection and welfare." "Members of the legislature tell us that if we could only make up our minds as to what we want we might get something."[1]

While there is much rivalry between the committees, yet to report them as always rivaling each other would not be fair. On the State Printing Bill of 1892, for example, the three committees joined in sending to every organization in the state a circular signed by the three chairmen asking their assistance, and the measure received the united support of the committees.

After the Federation was formed an attempt was made to distinguish between the measures of the new organization and other measures. The executive council called the attention of all legislators to the fact that no bill should be considered as a "labor measure" unless it should be espoused by the legislative committee. This has succeeded in cutting out the influence behind a large number of bills advocated by local unions. It could not very well affect the program of the other state organization. The year following (1899) the legislative commit-

[1] *Proceedings of the Workingmen's Assembly Convention*, 1894.

tee asked again for "power to place the official seal of condemnation on fake labor bills." The committee has adopted the policy of refusing to approve of any measure, even though it be a worthy one, coming from organizations not affiliated with the state organization.

Still other sources of confusion exist. There is the introduction of bills dealing with labor interests by persons not considered to be labor men, and even by legislators themselves. Even though these may be excellent measures, the labor leaders usually refuse to recognize them as such. They undoubtedly consider this attitude necessary for the maintenance of efficient organization and supervision. Yet this can not be said to be the full explanation of their attitude. They take a very well defined position in the matter. "More than half the labor bills introduced," they say, "are introduced for the purpose of giving the introducer political prestige in his district, or are introduced by scheming persons claiming to represent this or that labor organization, while the real object in view by the promoter is gain for himself." This is without doubt an unjustifiable accusation for any labor leader to make, yet it shows the determination to keep the initiation of laws in their own hands as much as possible. It also shows an unwarrantable impatience with others who have very often only a desire to promote the good of all.

Reference has been made to the plan of submitting pledges to candidates. After their election the idea is applied still further by keeping a careful record of all voting on labor bills. These results are embodied each year in the report of the legislative committee, and the legislators are classified according to their "records." Various classes have been made from time to time. In 1889 they were designated as "Special Mention,"

"Favorable Mention," "Black List" and "Dodgers." In 1891 they were "Special Mention," "Favorable Mention," "Luke Warm" and "Black List." In 1893, "Roll of Honor," "Special Mention," "Favorable Mention," "Luke Warm" and "Black List." The legislators were assigned places in these various lists according to the number of labor bills for which they had voted. Recently the plan has been changed by printing with each legislator's name the number of bills supported, the number opposed and the number of absences at the time of voting. Those having an unfavorable record are "remembered next fall when they ask for your suffrages in order to misrepresent you two years more." Even a "good record" is not always taken as favorable evidence. The committee know, as they report, of many cases where bills are "held back through subterfuge or excuse until the last days of the session. Then the member for the purpose of *making a record* will move the passage."

The committee is always in correspondence with local organizations, and this enables them at a critical point to draw in from local unions resolutions, letters or telegrams to members, and even special visits of delegations from some field where a doubtful vote may be turned or a hostile attitude modified.

An important addition to the system has been urged. It is the appointment of local legislative committees in the districts. The central committee at Albany would be in even more direct communication with these local committees than with the local unions. They would be the intermediate agencies for arousing local support or opposition. Experience has shown that a letter or a call from a member or delegation of a constituency has far more weight with a legislator than any pressure brought to bear from other sources. Through local committees advantage might be taken of this influence quickly and forcibly at those critical times when votes are needed and when other means of securing them have failed.

This is the outline of the system. In many points it is strong, in many it is weak. It is above all an intensely practical system. It aims to benefit labor and labor alone. It is suspicious of outside interference and jealous of suggestion. Its organization is becoming stronger as it is learning by experience. The demands of the future may be relied upon to modify its workings still further, and such modification will tend to eliminate the weak points and to strengthen those already strong. It may even now be regarded as a powerful influence in legislation. As to results in legislation, positive statements must be made with extreme caution. In general it may be said, beyond the possibility of contradiction, that the organization above described has been a potent factor in securing that body of laws known by the general name of labor legislation.[1]

While it cannot be doubted that positive influence has been exerted in securing legislation, great difficulty arises in determining the exact extent of that influence. So numerous and interwoven are the various interests

[1] Taking the laws that have been denominated labor laws by the state department of labor, I have traced their development in the session laws of the state, making at the same time a parallel study of the proceedings of the state Federation conventions and the work of their legislative committee. This study shows in a striking way both the activity of the labor organizations and their determined advocacy of the bills about to become laws. Many bills are drafted by the labor organizations and introduced directly as labor bills. Another fact that attests the influence of these organizations is that the governors of the state have more than once either made to the leaders direct offers of appointment to important offices or have consulted them as to what person to appoint.

represented in the legislative halls that to single out any one of them and make a mathematical calculation of its force is impossible. To attribute the passage of any given law to the influence of any single organization, or to that of a group of allied organizations, is wholly unsafe. Even the opposition of directly conflicting interests may enlist in favor of a movement interests which were at first neutral. In response to inquiries concerning particular measures, replies similar to the following have been received:

The bill for the inspection of mercantile establishments was first urged by the Consumers' League. It was endorsed by the Central Labor Union and other organizations and was vigorously pushed by the Working Women's Society. The Social Reform Club and thousands of working people, and moderate and immoderate radicals also aided in the passage of the bill. Five years were consumed in the struggle. The bill was indorsed by all the leading physicians in the city and was approved by many of the clergy.

Another inquiry was responded to as follows:

I have made inquiry about the matter . . . . . . Mr. A, President of B——, claims that they introduced the bill. Mr. C, Secretary of D——, says that they were the real cause of the bill. However, he does not deny that the bill was introduced this time by B——.

The study leads to the conclusion that in securing the enactment of the labor laws of the state, labor organizations have taken a very active interest and that as compared with other organizations, they have exercised the greatest and in most cases the determining influence.

CHAPTER IV

INDEPENDENT POLITICAL ACTION

It is not through neglect that organized labor has formulated no definite policy in relation to politics. In fact, it has often been stated in various ways that no broad general policy was attempted; that the conditions of the hour were alone to determine action. But whether such a policy be definitely outlined or not, the forces which are set in motion must necessarily yield results. The present chapter will consider what appear to be some of the more striking indications of the important influence which labor organizations may exert in politics. The conclusions reached are more or less tentative because the movement is comparatively new. It is hoped however that the advantages to be gained from a "play at the hazardous game of prophecy" fully warrant a consideration of the subject.

Even whether labor organizations should enter into politics at all, as organizations, is a question upon which there is decided disagreement. They firmly believe in drafting, presenting and urging with all their organized strength the passage of bills. But as has been shown above, the plan of organizing in local districts for making nominations has not met with much approval. Political action of a more general nature has, however, been much discussed.

The aims and objects of labor unions as expressed in numerous places by different organizations are many and various. Among them are to be found the following: "to raise wages;" "to shorten hours;" "to lessen excessive competition for situations;" "to educate as to public questions;" "to develop fraternity;" "a good investment" (social benefit); "to cheer the home and fireside;" "to lighten toil;" "to create rights and abolish wrongs;" "to develop manhood;" "to enlarge society;" "to foster education;" "to assist each other in any manner justifiable and with voluntary financial help in the event of a strike or lockout, when duly approved by the Executive Committee" (an application of "mutual assistance"—"one of the basic principles" of trade unionism); "to mould public opinion in favor of labor" (by mass meetings, a labor press and labor literature). In this entire catalogue two purposes appear in striking prominence. They relate to wages and to hours of labor. There is a noticeable absence of reference to political action. The most pronounced utterance touching upon political action appears in the constitution of the Workingmen's Federation, which reads: to "obtain the enactment of such measures by the state legislature as will be beneficial to us." This, together with the history of the formation of the Workingmen's Assembly, indicates a distinction in purpose between local and central unions on the one hand and the state organizations on the other. By far the greater part of the purposes quoted above are taken from local and central unions or national and international unions. The state organizations emphasize especially the importance of legislation, of further organization of locals and of closer union with central and state federations. Even separate political programs have been formulated as bases for party platforms. They include the subjects of legislation reviewed in chapter iii, and other subjects as well. The Workingmen's Federation, in 1899, declared for public ownership and operation of all means of transportation, of the telegraph and telephone systems, and of gas, electric and water plants, and the establishing of labor bureaus in the different labor centres of the state under the control of trade unions. At other times the program has included "equal pay for equal work for both sexes," the demand that "the government shall issue all currency or money without intervention of banking corporations," and other measures of which the list is a long one.

The actual and practical relations with politics gives rise to the greatest difference of opinion. Two resolutions of the American Federation of Labor touching this point are significant.

That as our efforts are centered against all forms of industrial slavery and economic wrong, we must also direct our economic energies to remove all forms of political servitude and party slavery, to the end that the working people may act as a unit at the polls at every election. That the American Federation of Labor most firmly and unequivocally favors the independent use of the ballot by the trade unionists and working men, united regardless of party, that we may elect men from our own ranks to make new laws and administer them along the lines laid down in the legislative demands of the American Federation of Labor, and at the same time secure an impartial judiciary that will not govern us by arbitrary injunctions of the courts, nor act as the pliant tools of corporate wealth.

In 1887 a resolution was presented to the convention that read as follows:

WHEREAS, This is not a political body, and should not identify itself with any party or the men of any party; therefore, be it

Resolved, That it is the sense of this Assembly that no mention should be made of any man in any party that can be used as political capital to influence the vote of the people.

This resolution was rejected. A year earlier than this the president, in his address, declared it to be his belief that "political action is just as essential to success in labor matters as is the sun to the budding plant. . . . Therefore I am opposed to the proposition to abandon politics in connection with our organization."

In 1898 a resolution was introduced in the convention calling upon the workingmen of the state "to enter a political movement irrespective of the present existing parties, so as to secure legislation beneficial to themselves instead of asking such from those who are in the employ of their enemies." The committee, in reporting this resolution, recommended that "it should not be brought before the body at this time," a time when more thorough amalgamation was being attempted. The resolution was not adopted. During all this difference of opinion the practical policy has continued to be that outlined by the president in the address of 1887 as being the policy of the past: "To elect labor men to offices wherever and whenever an opportunity presented itself. When it did not, then to stand by the men who stood by our measures, and defeat those who opposed them." It seems altogether probable that the policy will continue to be that of uniting the labor vote of the community and casting it in favor of the best candidate from the point of view of labor, relying on success in enough districts in the state to give labor a fair representation in the legislature. It is not likely that any conscious change will be made, but it is probable that events themselves will modify the workings of the plan so as to secure greater efficiency. Strong party ties favoring the existing parties will not allow of a further departure, and the expenses to be met in forming a new party organization is an additional and very practical obstacle.

Laboring men are more pronounced in stating the end to be secured by their legislation than any other group that appears before the legislature. Legislation "beneficial to us" says the constitution. "To secure legislation beneficial to ourselves" is a characteristic utterance. The legislators who stand by "our measures" are "friends," and those who oppose them are "enemies." The idea seems to prevail, and there can be no doubt that there has been much to substantiate it, that all who are not for them and for them alone are against them. Short-range contact with practical politics has done much to fix this idea. Yet if the attitude of laboring men were less directly one of self-interest, and if they were to recognize both in theory and in practice other interests or their own broader interests, they would unquestionably receive far heartier approval from the community at large.

It is the often-expressed opinion of labor leaders that a legislator, once seated by the labor vote, has no discretion upon measures coming before him for consideration. This appears again and again in resolutions, petitions, addresses and written articles. Resolutions passed frequently and without question by conventions have a very imperative tone. "Resolved, That the Workingmen's Assembly demand from the legislature to pass a law. . . . " "That we demand of the present legislature the passage of an act . . . " "That this Assembly demand the present legislature to pass the bill introduced [calling for another standing committee], to whom all bills for our benefit shall be referred." Another resolution condemns the custom of attaching amendments to labor bills and directs the legislative committee "not to permit any such action." "If we have men from our ranks in the legislative halls of the state," says the report of 1899, "they should willingly carry out your mandates, and regardless of party affiliation make the fight for labor's rights hand in hand." It appears that they not only may dictate to the representatives elected by them, but that they may, in their opinion, issue demands to the entire legislative body and rely upon the ballot to make "legislative enemies feel our power to punish and legislative friends with equal force feel our friendship." This attitude not only sharply distinguishes between a representative and a delegate, but reduces the delegate to a mere automaton, useless except as a legally necessary form to stamp drafted bills as laws.

While many of these resolutions sound harsh and overbearing, this can hardly be said to be intentional on the part of those who introduce them. Compared with the resolutions of earlier years there has been decided improvement. Experience has done much for those who conduct the affairs of the unions, and it is not entirely their own fault that they have been obliged to rely on experience as their only teacher. The early gains were made at the expense of so great a struggle and in the face of such general opposition that it is not at all strange that when any gain was made the labor unionist viewed it as his own and one of which he was fully entitled to take advantage. Even a legislator once seated by efforts of the labor-union vote was not sure to remain true to his constituency. As one leader has expressed it, they sometimes experience a change of heart after a few days of service as legislators. This danger prompts the leaders to keep careful watch of their "friends" to see that their hearts are kept true to the cause. Further, it is not at all to be wondered at that plans for independent political action were advocated. The struggle to gain their ends was often a discouraging one. Existing party organizations were slow to listen. Some things were gained by united action. What more natural than the conclusion that if an organization were formed it could act independently, and could secure for those concerned the realization of their ideals?

While there are evidences of conflicting opinion on the question of independent political action, there are very strong practical considerations that hold in check any extensive movement in that direction. It soon becomes obvious to any labor leader who contemplates a thorough-going political organization that such an organization cannot be bound together by so slender a cord as a labor-law program affords. Since this is the only force holding the men together in the midst of numerous and powerful forces tending to draw them apart, it is not found sufficient. As a result the first campaign brings into action those powerful forces of long-standing party affiliation and of deep-seated feeling, and the cherished organization is dissolved. In recognition of the difficulties of forming a new party organization a second plan is often tried. This plan consists in turning the men into a party already formed. This has far less chance of permanent success even than the former plan, because of the feeling of hostility in the minds of so many men towards any party but their own. This feeling is often very bitter. In spite of the fact that this plan can never be fully achieved, efforts are continually being made to secure a temporary gain. Hardly a convention is now held in which an effort is not made to "steal" the convention for one of the political parties. This has provoked such acute watchfulness that often a very important matter is completely blocked because of a suspicion that some delegate is after "political capital."

These experiences are teaching the most reliable and conservative leaders that the only safe plan to follow is to confine attention closely to strictly labor affairs and to avoid anything that suggests in the remotest way independent political action.

CHAPTER V

THE DEVELOPMENT OF THE LAW OF CONSPIRACY

ALTHOUGH there is a difference in the legal theory of the origin of conspiracy in the English and in the American law, yet in its application by the courts of the two countries there has been no fundamental difference. Beginning, in England, with the statutes regulating trade organizations, conspiracy was held to be of statute law origin. At the close of the sixteenth century there began the development of the idea that as between the combination to do the criminal acts and the acts themselves, the gist of the conspiracy was in the agreement or combination; that even where the proposed acts were statutory offences the conspiracy to do them might be held and punished as a substantive crime at common law.[1] Thus, at the time that the colonists in America were developing their law on English precedents, conspiracy was held to be a crime at common law.[2] In this way the common law came to be the basis for the early decisions in New York. Throughout the entire development of the court law, English decisions have been frequently cited and English legal authorities quoted in support of the attitude taken by the courts of the state. This attitude has not been one of entire dependence, however, for sev-

[1] Wright, *Law of Criminal Conspiracies*, pp. 5-15.

[2] For discussion of the common-law origin of conspiracy, see Carson, in Wright on *Law of Criminal Conspiracies*, p. 95; also, State *v.* Buchanan, Ct. of App. of Md., 5 Harris and Johnson (Md.), 317 (1821).

eral cases show that distinctions were made because the statute laws of England had no binding force in America, and because the conditions prevailing in America demanded a different application.[1]

In the early history of the state there was no statute regulating disputes between laborers and their employers. Conspiracy, however, was a question that had to be dealt with in the first years of statehood, and this necessity influenced both the form taken by the law and its later application to labor disputes. It was a necessity arising not from labor troubles, but from conditions quite foreign to such disputes. These events gave a peculiar turn to the statement of the law.

During the Revolutionary struggle persons favorably disposed toward the cause of England became very active, and it was necessary to watch them closely. Acts intended to militate against the interests of the state were considered as acts of conspiracy. The state convention during the war appointed a special commission for the purpose of "enquiring into, detecting and defeating all conspiracies which might be formed in this state against the liberties of America." Experience showed this commission to be "of great use and importance." The commission was continued by the first session of the legislature in 1778,[2] and remained throughout the war. In 1783, by act of March 27, the prisoners and all pending cases then in the hands of the commission were

[1] "The decisions of the English courts upon questions affecting the rights of workmen ought, at least, to be received with caution, in view of the fact that the latter ones are largely supported by earlier precedents which were entirely consistent with the policy of the statute law of England, but are hostile not only to the statute law of this country, but to the spirit of our institutions." Chief Justice Parker, 170 N. Y., 332.

[2] L., 1778, ch. 3.

turned over to the justices of the peace. A suspected person could then be called before a justice of the peace and held accountable to that officer. Thus the state attempted to suppress conspiracies against "the liberties of America" while the war was in progress. In 1801 a different idea appears. On March 30 an act was passed to prevent and punish champerty and maintenance. This act was apparently aimed at the prevalence of false accusations and charges and at efforts to "get business" by sharing the gains. It seems not unreasonable to suppose that this law resulted largely from persecution of the Tories and efforts to deprive them of their property because of their adherence to the cause of England during the war. The substance of the law of 1801 is as follows:

All persons who confederate by oath, agreement or other alliance, falsely and maliciously to indict, or cause to be indicted any person, or falsely to move and maintain any plea or suit, shall be adjudged conspirators, and all persons who move pleas and suits, or cause them to be moved, either by their own procurement or by others, and sue them at their own proper costs, for to have part of the land or thing in controversy or demand, or part of the gains, shall be adjudged champertors . . . . No person, by himself or by any other, shall take upon himself to maintain quarrels of others, to the let and disturbance of law, upon pain of being punished by fine or imprisonment.[1]

This law was repeated *in toto* in the revised laws of 1813. It remained unchanged until 1828, when a revision of the statutes included the following law pertaining to conspiracy. It is quoted in full to make clear the then prevailing idea of conspiracy and for purposes of comparison with later statements:

[1] L., 1801, ch. 87.

Section 8. If two or more persons shall conspire, either, 1. To commit any offence; or, 2. Falsely and maliciously to indict another for any offence, or to procure another to be charged or arrested for any such offence; or, 3. Falsely to move or maintain any suit; or, 4. To cheat and defraud any person of any property by any means which are in themselves criminal; or, 5. To cheat and defraud any person of any property by any means which, if executed, would amount to a cheat, or to obtaining money or property by false pretences; or, 6. To commit any act injurious to the public health, to public morals, or to trade or commerce; or for the perversion or obstruction of justice or the due administration of the laws: They shall be deemed guilty of a misdemeanor.

Section 9. No conspiracies, other than such as are enumerated in the last section, are punishable criminally.

Section 10. No agreement, except to commit a felony upon the person of another, or to commit arson or burglary, shall be deemed a conspiracy, unless some act beside such agreement be done to effect the object thereof by one or more parties to such agreement.[1]

In recommending this section of the revised statutes the commission stated:

The preceding enumeration includes all the cases usually considered as conspiracy except that of a conspiracy to injure an individual by means not in themselves criminal. . . . Under these circumstances, and without reference to what may be supposed to be the existing law, the revisors have prepared the above section as containing all that is expedient to be enumerated.

The commission added a clause to its recommendation which the legislature refused to accept. This clause was to make it criminal to conspire "to defraud or injure any

[1] R. S., 1828, pt. 4, ch. 1, tit. 6, secs. 8, 9, 10.

person in his trade or business." Concerning the 9th section, the revisors remarked that it was "necessary [in order] to put at rest the doubts and difficulties respecting the common law offences." Of the 10th section the revisors said:

> By a metaphysical train of reasoning, which has never been adopted in any other case in the whole criminal law, the offence of conspiracy is made to consist in the intent; in an act of the mind; and to prevent the shock to common-sense which such a proposition would be sure to produce, the formation of this intent by an interchange of thoughts is made itself an overt act, done in pursuance of that interchange or agreement. . . . Acts and deeds are the subjects of human laws; not thoughts and intents unless accompanied by acts.[1]

The opinion has been expressed that the legislature in rejecting the clause, "to defraud or injure any person in his trade or business," acted wisely, since they put an end to the vague generalizations of the common law.[2]

At this point it may be noted that the New York state law rests primarily upon a basis of common law enforced by such statutes as have been referred to, enacted at the time of the Revolutionary War. These Revolutionary influences remained dominant until about 1813, and gave the appearance of a statute-law basis to conspiracy. After the particular evils against which these laws were aimed had become less obvious, the common-law basis began to assert itself again and it was felt that conspiracy was without question indictable at common law. The revision of 1828 made this change: it gathered up from the common law those principles upon which at the

[1] 9 Cowan, 624–5.

[2] *Fifth Annual Report of the Bureau of Labor Statistics, N. Y.* (1887), p. 653.

time it seemed desirable to base action against conspiracy and expressed them definitely in statute form, thus making the basis again a statute-law basis. From 1828 down to 1870, the provisions remained unchanged, although several revisions of the statutes as a whole were made.

In 1870 the legislature passed a statute which considerably modified the whole section dealing with conspiracy so far as the laborer was concerned. This law read as follows:

The provisions [of the Revised Statutes] shall not be construed in any court of this state to restrict or prohibit the orderly and peaceable assembling or co-operation of persons employed in any profession, trade or handicraft, for the purpose of securing an advance in the rate of wages or compensation, or for the maintenance of such rate.[1]

This law was in a later revision embodied in the conspiracy section and in 1881 the whole subject of conspiracy was transferred to the penal code. After some changes in wording, the section was made to read as follows:

Section 168. If two or more persons conspire, either, 1. To commit a crime; or, 2. Falsely and maliciously to indict another for a crime, or to procure another to be complained of or arrested for a crime; or, 3. Falsely to institute or maintain an action or special proceeding; or, 4. To cheat or defraud another out of property, by any means which are in themselves criminal, or which, if executed, would amount to a cheat, or to obtain money or any other property by false pretenses; or, 5. To prevent another from exercising a lawful trade or calling, or doing any other lawful act by force, threats, intimidation, or by interfering or threatening to interfere with tools,

[1] L., 1870, ch. 19.

implements, or property belonging to or used by another, or with the use or employment thereof; or, 6. To commit any act injurious to the public health, to public morals, or to trade or commerce, or for the perversion or obstruction of justice or of the due administration of the laws: Each of them is guilty of a misdemeanor.

Section 170. No conspiracy is punishable criminally unless it is one of those enumerated in the last two sections [168 and 169], and the orderly and peaceable assembling or co-operation of persons employed in any calling, trade, or handicraft, for the purpose of obtaining an advance in the rate of wages or compensation, or for maintaining such rate, is not a conspiracy, if none of the acts or things prohibited thereby is done or agreed to be done by the persons assembling or co-operating.

Section 171. No agreement except to commit a felony upon the person of another, or to commit arson or burglary amounts to a conspiracy, unless some act besides such an agreement be done to effect the object thereof, by one or more of the parties to such agreement.[1]

Section 171 A. Any person or persons, employer or employers of labor, and any person or persons of any corporation or corporations on behalf of such corporation or corporations who shall hereafter coerce or compel any person or persons, employe or employes, laborer or mechanic, to enter into an agreement either written or verbal from such person, persons, employe, laborer, or mechanic not to join or become a member of any labor organization as a condition of such person or persons securing employment, or continuing in the employment of any such person or persons, employer or employers, corporation or corporations, shall be deemed guilty of a misdemeanor.[2]

[1] P. C., tit. viii, ch. viii, being ch. 676 of the laws of 1881, passed July 26, 1881.

[2] L., 1887, ch. 688.

That this legislation has been accomplished in part through the efforts of organized labor appears from the following evidence taken from the reports of annual conventions. It stands as evidence of further discussion and of other activity outside of conventions enlisted in an effort to arouse public opinion in favor of legislation less hostile to the interests of labor.

In 1869 and 1870 were held the first of the series of annual conventions of the state labor organization known as the Workingmen's Assembly. In the annual addresses of the president before these conventions[1] attention was continually called to the disadvantageous position of the laboring man due to the indefinite provisions of the conspiracy law. Many cases were cited where charges had been brought against laboring men and punishment visited upon them for conspiracy when, if we may rely upon the accuracy of the knowledge of the president, their only purpose had been to secure better wages or shorter hours or improved conditions of labor. For example, several members of a bricklayers' union had refused to work with an unindentured apprentice. The matter was carried to the supreme court as a conspiracy case. Another strike of bricklayers in New York City was taken to the courts and the men charged with conspiracy. During 1868, says the president in one of his reports, "several members of the trade unions of this state have been called upon to appear in court and answer to the charge of violating the statutes relating to trade and commerce as criminals and conspirators." One of the charges he quotes as follows: "Conspiracy and combination in refusing to work for a man employing an unindentured apprentice." This case was decided

[1] *Proceedings, Workingmen's Assembly*, 1869.

in the lower courts in favor of the plaintiff. It seems to have been the view of the president that this law was revived for the special purpose of preventing laborers from asserting their rights. "During the past year a law has been found on the statute books making workingmen's associations a conspiracy." The law came to light upon the arrest and indictment of members of trade unions "for carrying out the principles of their constitution and laws." The convention of the Assembly willingly took the matter up upon the recommendation of the president and drafted resolutions against the enforcement of this provision and the repeal of the law. "Whereas," reads one of the resolutions,

Some antiquarians having found a law on the statute books of this state, so-called conspiracy; and, Whereas, Said law is capable of being construed to the detriment of the working men of this state, by preventing them from combining for their mutual protection and benefit; Resolved, That this Assembly respectfully ask, in the name of twenty-five thousand workingmen, the repeal of said law.

Another resolution was as follows:

Resolved that this organization use every endeavor in its power with the Legislature of this state to have erased from the statute books all laws that may infringe on the rights of labor, especially that entitled the Conspiracy Law, rendering workingmen liable to be prosecuted in asserting and maintaining their rights.

The convention also adopted the draft of a bill which they instructed their committee to urge upon the legislature. This bill read as follows:

Section 1. It shall be lawful for any and all classes of

mechanics, journeymen, tradesmen and laborers to form societies and associations for their mutual aid, benefit and protection, and peaceably to meet, discuss and establish all necessary by-laws, rules and regulations to carry out the same.

Section 2. The provisions [of the Revised Statutes] shall not apply to the members of any society or association formed in pursuance of this act.[1]

This bill, known as the Conspiracy Bill, was presented in the session of 1869, and killed in committee of the senate after having been passed by the assembly. Although nothing was accomplished in 1869, the fact that at the very next session the provision in Chapter 19, which has been referred to above, was passed, indicates that the action of the labor organizations had more influence than at first appeared.

[1] *Workingmen's Assembly, Proceedings*, 1869.

CHAPTER VI

JUDICIAL DECISIONS—THE RIGHT TO STRIKE—BEFORE 1890

THE earliest reported decision bearing on this subject was not in New York state, but it was a case which had some influence on later decisions. The case was that of the boot and shoe makers of Philadelphia, tried in the mayor's court in that city in 1806.[1] The conclusions to which the court comes may be stated briefly as follows: "A combination of workmen to raise their wages may be considered in a two-fold point of view; one is to benefit themselves, the other is to injure those who do not join their society. The rule of law condemns both."

The next case of importance was in 1809 in New York state.[2] The case was an indictment found against the journeymen cordwainers of New York. This case charged "a conspiracy with the features of an unlawful club, rules and by-laws; refusal to work or to let others work; threats and conspiracy to prejudice and impoverish by indirect means master shoemakers, and to hinder workmen who had broken their rules from following

[1] The pamphlet containing a report of this case (*The Trial of the Boot and Shoe Makers of Philadelphia*, Phila., 1806) is very scarce, but a very full account of the case is given in Wright, *The Law of Criminal Conspiracies*, p. 145.

[2] Case of the Journeymen Cordwainers of the City of New York. *Select Cases Adjudged in the Courts of the State of New York*, vol. i, p. 111. Printed and published by Isaac Riley, 1811. Also, People *v.* Melvin, 2 Wheeler Cr. Cases, 262. The quotation is from the summary in Wright, *Law of Criminal Conspiracies*, p. 149.

their art." As this is the earliest recorded case in New York state, it is of historical interest, but as illustrating principles it was not important. The mayor charged the jury in this case as follows:

There were two points of view in which the offence of a conspiracy might be considered; the one where there existed a combination to do an act unlawful in itself, to the prejudice of other persons; the other where the act done, or the object of it, was not unlawful, but unlawful means were used to accomplish it. As to the first, there would be no doubt that a combination to do an unlawful act was a conspiracy. The second depended on the common principle, that the goodness of the end would not justify improper means to obtain it. . . . The court did not mean to say, nor did the facts in the case require them to decide, whether an agreement not to work except for certain wages would amount to this offence, without any unlawful means taken to enforce it. . . . When the society determined on any measure, it found no difficulty in carrying it into execution. If its ordinary functions failed, it enforced obedience by decreeing what was called a strike against a particular shop that had transgressed, or a general turn-out against all the shops in the city. These steps were generally decisive, and compelled submission in all concerned. Whatever might be the motives of the defendants, or their object, the means thus employed were arbitrary and unlawful, and their having been directed against several individuals in the present case, it was brought, in the opinion of the court, within one of the descriptions of the offence which had been given.

Although this case did not decide definitely that a combination of workmen was necessarily a conspiracy, it did hold that a strike was unlawful.

The next important case was People *v.* Trequier in 1823. In this case the defendants were accused of conspiring to refuse to work for any master hatter "who had in his service any workmen or journeymen engaged in the said art who had not agreed to certain rules adopted by" the defendants. The evidence in this case showed that the master hatters of the city had had a meeting to agree to reduce wages. To counteract this agreement among employers the journeymen had formed a society, and had agreed not to work under a certain price. It was shown that the defendants had objected to work "severally at different times, but at one time at least they all together objected to work." The defendants offered to prove a conspiracy among the master hatters not to employ any journeyman who left his last place on account of wages in order to prove that the meeting of the journeymen was for a lawful purpose. The evidence was not allowed. The defendants also contended that the case was not unlike an earlier agreement of grocers and others not to purchase goods of auctioneers. In the decision of the court the following definition of conspiracy was stated as fundamental: "An agreement or combination between two or more persons to do an unlawful act or to accomplish a purpose lawful in itself by means that are criminal or unlawful." The meeting of grocers was for a lawful purpose—for the general advantage of the community. The case before the court was held to show conspiracy to be against the prosecutor alone, and resulted in forcing him from his shop and from his business. Referring to the association of masters, the court held that "one conspiracy cannot justify another." The jury, being thus charged, decided against the defendants.

At the end of this case is appended a note which gives a summary of the cases on conspiracy:

The law relating to conspiracy has undergone a great alteration within a few centuries past. It was taken formerly in a more confined and limited extent than it is at present. The most usual method [against conspiracy] is now by indictment and is a most extensive remedy, embracing almost every possible case of combination.

A variety of illustrations of conspiracy are then cited, among which are the following:

Journeymen confederating and refusing to work unless for certain wages may be indicted for a conspiracy. . . . The offence consists in the conspiracy and not in the refusal, and all conspiracies are illegal though the subject matter of them may be lawful. Journeymen may each singly refuse to work, but if they refuse by preconcert or association they may be indicted for conspiracy. If several go to the theatre by previous agreement to hiss an actor or cry down a play they are guilty of conspiracy. A combination and agreement between . . . officers to resign is unlawful. A combination to raise the price by false rumors is indictable. In conspiracy the crime is completed by the unlawful agreement. No positive or direct evidence need be given of the fact of conspiring but may be inferred from the circumstances of the case. The gist of a conspiracy is the unlawful confederacy and the offence is completed when the confederacy is made, and any act done in pursuit of it is no constituent part of the offence. An indictment for a conspiracy to the prejudice of people generally without naming an individual can be supported. It is unnecessary for a prosecution for a conspiracy to show that any step was taken by the conspirators or either of them towards the consummation of the act agreed to be done. It is sufficient if an agreement to do some unlawful or immoral act existed.

In connection with each of these statements, cases are cited or authorities quoted in evidence of the principle.

The statements show the status of court law on conspiracy as late as 1823. Although many of the cases are English cases, yet the connection between the New York courts and English law is so intimate that they are in substance a part of the court law of the state. People *v.* Trequier was the last case of importance before the New York courts previous to the revision of the statutes.

In 1835 came the first case based upon the new law relating to trade and commerce.[1] It was a leading case and has often been cited in cases involving a similar principle. It was charged that journeymen had united in "an unlawful club and combination" to prevent journeymen bootmakers in Geneva from working below certain rates "prescribed by the defendants" "to the great injury of the trade of the state of New York." A fine of ten dollars was imposed by the organization on any one who made a pair of coarse shoes for less than one dollar, and the defendants refused to work for any master employing such journeymen. One Pennock made shoes for one Lum in Geneva for seventy-five cents and refused to pay the fine, consequently the journeymen refused to work for any one employing Pennock. The decision of the court after quoting the law of conspiracy from the revised statutes raised the question: Is a conspiracy to raise wages an act injurious to trade and commerce? This is the essence of the case, for the mere raising of wages is in itself no offense. An agreement, held the court, among journeymen to raise wages is a matter of public concern. Common law holds it indictable by English legal adjudications. Continuing the development of the argument, the justice next entered upon a discussion of the economics involved in the question:

[1] People *v.* Fisher.

Whatever disputes may exist among political economists upon the point, I think there can be no doubt, in a legal sense, but what the wages of labor compose a material portion of the value of manufactured articles. The products of mechanical labor compose a large proportion of the materials with which trade is carried on. . . . If journeymen bootmakers, by extravagant demands for wages, so enhance the price for boots made in Geneva, for instance, that boots made elsewhere, in Auburn, for example, can be sold cheaper, is not such an act injurious to trade? It is surely so to the trade of Geneva in that particular article, and that, I apprehend, is all that is necessary to bring the offence within the statute. It is important to the best interests of society that the price of labor be left to regulate itself, or rather be limited by the demand for it. Combinations and confederacies to enhance or reduce the prices of labor, or of any articles of trade or commerce, are injurious. They may be oppressive by compelling the public to give more for an article of necessity or of convenience than it is worth, or, on the other hand, of compelling the labor of the mechanic for less than its value.

Demand and supply will properly regulate wages as well as the price of articles, but, "the right does not exist either to enhance the price of the article, or the wages of the mechanic, by any forced or artificial means." A laborer "may say that he will not make coarse boots for less than one dollar per pair, but he has no right to say that no other mechanic shall make them for less," any more than a cloth merchant may dictate the price of the cloth another has to sell.

If one individual does not possess such a right over the conduct of another, no number of individuals can possess such a right. All combinations, therefore, to effect such an object are injurious, not only to the individual particularly oppressed but to the public at large. In the present case an industrious man was driven out of employment by the unlawful measures pursued by the defendants, and an injury done to the community by diminishing the quantity of productive labor and of internal trade. In so far as the individual sustains an injury, the remedy by indictment is taken away by our Revised Statutes, and the sufferer is left to his action on the case, but in so far as the public are concerned, in the embarrassment of trade by the discouragement of industry, the defendants are liable to punishment by indictment.

The decision then argued that if combinations are legal in Geneva, they are so in every other place, and if a limit may be put at one dollar, it may be put at ten dollars or fifty dollars, and "no man can wear a pair of boots without giving such price as the journeymen bootmakers may choose to require. This I apprehend would be a monopoly of the most odious kind." What one trade may do, all trades may do, leading to "derangement and confusion," which is unquestionably "injurious to trade." While no great danger is imminent, yet, if when "universally or even generally entered into they would be prejudicial to trade and to the public, they are wrong in each particular case."

The truth is that industry requires no such means to support it. Competition is the life of trade. If defendants cannot make coarse boots for less than one dollar per pair, let them refuse to do so; but let them not directly or indirectly undertake to say that others shall not do the work for a less price. . . . The interference of the defendants was unlawful; its tendency is not only to individual oppression, but to public inconvenience and embarrassment.

The next important case was Master Stevedores' Association *v.* Walsh, 1867. This case is of importance for more reasons than one. It makes a careful study of previous cases and the authorities cited by them. It is comprehensive in its view, showing a clear understanding of the social problems involved. Further, it shows an appreciation of the importance of organizations of laborers and their possibilities when well conducted. A corporation, the Master Stevedores' Association, adopted a by-law that there should be no variation from the prices established by the association, and that any member found guilty of working for less than the fixed price should forfeit to the association twenty-five per cent of the wages. This forfeit was to be collectible in the name of the corporation by due process of law. The defendant in the case had subscribed to this agreement in joining the association, and had worked in violation of the above-cited rule. He was fined one hundred and twenty-five dollars, and action was brought for its recovery. The demurrer was that the by-law was illegal because the object designed to be effected was one forbidden by law. People *v.* Fisher was the leading case relied upon, the principles of which have already been referred to. This case was examined fully by the court, and the justice declined to accept it as conclusive even on the principle involved in that case. A very full review was made in the written decision. First, the distinguishing features of each case were pointed out and contrasted. Even admitting that the principle involved was the same, the court differed with the line of reasoning which People *v.* Fisher adopted. After summing up the case, the court commented as follows:

Much of what is here said is undoubtedly right and it is forcibly put. Many of the reasons were applicable to the case before the court, which was correctly determined in accordance with the adjudged cases. The objection, however, is, that some of the propositions stated are not tenable, and that there is an omission throughout, to distinguish between what is entirely lawful for either journeymen or master workmen to do in their collective capacity, upon the subject of wages, and those unlawful combinations where the object is to control the rate of wages by the use of coercive means. It is not, nor has it ever been, a rule of the common law that any mutual agreement among journeymen for the purpose of raising their wages, is an indictable offence, or that they are guilty of a conspiracy if, by preconcert or arrangement, they refuse to work unless they receive an advance of wages.

The citations made by People *v.* Fisher were held to be unreliable; based on English statutes regulating wages; not applicable to American colonial conditions, and therefore not a part of the colonial law adopted by the state in 1777. In 1821 Chief Justice Gibson had declared that "it had never been decided in England that it was unlawful for journeymen to agree that they would not work, except for certain wages, or for master workmen to agree that they would not employ any journeymen, except at certain rates." The court then stated: "In corroboration of the statement of this very accurate and eminent jurist, I would add that I have examined down to the present time, and found no case, either in this country or in England, in which any such decision has been rendered." Such reference as has been made in previous cases the court held to have been made

simply by way of illustration, as there was no such question in the case, and was evidently made without examination, as no authorities are referred to. . . . In the New York Cordwainers' Case, after an elaborate argument of the question, the court declared that they would not say that an agreement not to work except for certain wages would amount to a conspiracy, without unlawful means were resorted to, to enforce it. This case was tried in this city [New York] in 1809. Judge Radcliffe, an eminent judge of the Supreme Court, was on the bench, having associated with him another distinguished judge, Josiah Hoffman, and their united opinion upon such a question, after it had been learnedly discussed before them by four of the ablest counsel then in this state . . . is entitled to more consideration than the opinion, expressed by way of illustration, by Justice Gross, or the passing observation of Recorder Levy.

After examining the opinions of the courts in New York, Pennsylvania and Massachusetts, the case next considered the English opinion:

The distinction [made by the English statute] between the legality of associations among workmen for the protection of their interests, by agreeing as a body not to work below certain prices, and illegal combination formed for the purpose of making it compulsory upon all the journeymen in a particular branch of business, and upon the employers to conform to certain prices by imposing penalties upon the journeymen in a city or town who refuse to do so, or by agreeing as a body not to work for any employer who will employ such a journeyman, or one who will not pay the penalty or become a member of the combination, or who seeks to accomplish such a purpose by violence, intimidation, or other unlawful means, is one that has been slowly arrived at in England, and toward which the courts in this country have been gradually approximating, for the reason that it has its foundation in the plainest principles of justice.

This condition, in the justice's opinion, gives rise to no apprehensions that employers will be at the mercy of their workmen. The history of English legislation shows that arbitrary control of the price of labor is futile, and the same must inevitably be the result in this country.

The truth of this was then pointed out by a more extended course of reasoning.

In summing up the previous cases, the judge concluded :

> It may, therefore, be laid down as the result of this examination, that it is lawful for any number of journeymen or of master workmen to agree, on the one part that they will not work below certain rates, or on the other that they will not pay above certain prices; but that any association or combination for the purpose of compelling journeymen or employers to conform to any rule, regulation, or agreement fixing the rate of wages to which they are not parties, by the imposition of penalties, by agreeing to quit the service of any employer who employs a journeyman below certain rates, unless the journeyman pays the penalty imposed by the combination, or by menaces, threats or intimidations, violence, or other unlawful means, is a conspiracy for which the parties entering into it may be indicted.

This rule was the outgrowth of a long series of cases, and was set forth for the first time as concluding a comprehensive examination of previous decisions.

In 1880, a warning note was sounded regarding the application of the law of 1870. Referring to this law the court held:

> This statute does not permit an association, or trades union so-called, or any body of men in the aggregate, to do any act which each one of such persons in his individual capacity and acting independently had not a right to do before the act was passed. This act does not shield a person from liability for his action in intimidating or coercing a fellow-laborer so that he shall leave his employer's service.[1]

In considering how far the law of 1828 had been modified by the statute of 1870, Judge Barrett said:

[1] Johnston Harvesting Company *v.* Meinhardt.

Formerly a conspiracy of working men to raise the rate of wages was criminally condemned as an act injurious to trade or commerce. But now it has been legislatively decreed that the orderly and peaceable assembling or co-operation of persons employed in any calling, trade or handicraft, for the purpose of obtaining an advance in the rate of wages and compensation, or of maintaining such rate, is not a conspiracy. This is what laboring men may lawfully do. What they may not do is to combine together for the purpose of preventing other people from working at prices to suit themselves.[1]

In another part of the same case this judge said:

A number of men may combine together to obtain larger wages for themselves in any employment. They may stop working if the employer unjustly refuses to accede to their just demands. So far they are right. They may also do their utmost, by speech, writing, suasion, appeal, and in any other lawful way, to persuade their fellow workingmen not to fill their places, nor to aid the employer in his unjust attitude. But the very moment that other men, disregarding all appeals and entreaties, find it to their own interest to fill the vacant places, they may not be stopped by violence, threats or intimidation. The moment workingmen resort to violence to prevent their brethren from filling the vacant places, the combination becomes criminal, and organized labor becomes organized law-breaking.

In 1886 this principle was carried still further.[2] The mere fact that no violence was used was not conclusive. It was not even necessary that there should be a direct threat. It was sufficient if the jury believed that the attitude actually presented by the distributers of the circulars by those who were defendants in the suit

[1] People *v.* Wilzig.

[2] People *v.* Kostka.

was one of intimidation, either to passers-by or to the proprietor of the business.

An important step was taken in 1887 in People *ex rel.* Gill *v.* Smith. This case admitted the legality of a peaceful strike entered upon to affect wages, but

> where there is no relation, direct or indirect, between the rate of wages and a strike, the combination which brings the latter about for unlawful purposes is a criminal conspiracy. The unlawful purpose of a strike may be evidenced by force, threats or intimidation to prevent another from exercising a lawful trade or calling.

If any arbitrary date can be fixed for the change at all, it may be said that 1885–1890 marks the change from the appeal for conviction for conspiracy to the appeal for the granting of an injunction. Before considering cases that have been before the courts since 1890, a summary may be made of the cases decided previous to that date. It cannot be done better than in the words of Carson:[1]

> The result of all the cases, ignoring matters of detail or special circumstances, appears to be as follows: Workmen may combine lawfully for their own protection and common benefit, for the advancement of their own interests, for the development of skill in their trade, or to prevent overcrowding therein, or to encourage those belonging to their trade to enter their guild; for the purpose of raising their wages or to secure a benefit which they can claim by law. The moment, however, that they proceed by threats, intimidation, violence, obstruction, or molestation, in order to secure their ends; or where their object be to impoverish third persons, or to extort money from their employers, or to ruin their business, or to encourage strikes or breaches of contract among others, or to restrict the freedom of others for the purpose of com-

[1] Wright, *Law of Criminal Conspiracies*, p. 178.

pelling employers to conform to their views, or to attempt to enforce rules upon those not members of their association, they render themselves liable to indictment. The rights of workmen are conceded, but the exercise of free-will and freedom of action within the limits of the law is also secured equally to the masters.

To this may be added the statement from Wharton, to the effect that, in case of no statute regulating the question "the day is passed when either in England or in the United States a court is justified in pronouncing indictable a combination of laborers agreeing in furtherance of this combination only to work at prices fixed by themselves."[1] Two reasons are assigned for this attitude: (1) The liberty of the laborer to adjust his business relations depending on the consent of the parties influenced by the conditions of the market can not be limited nor interfered with. (2) Any principle which could prevent the combination of employees would also prevent combinations of capital.

Thus, it appears that before 1890 it had been pretty definitely determined that an organized strike, if peaceable and for a lawful purpose, was not a conspiracy. This does not mean, however, that the question of the right to strike was settled. No sooner had the law been developed, as traced above, than new cases arose involving new questions. The decisions in these cases and the law developed by them will be the subject of the next chapter.

[1] *Criminal Law*, vol. ii, § 1366.

CHAPTER VII

JUDICIAL DECISIONS—THE RIGHT TO STRIKE—SINCE 1890

DURING the last decade of the past century a change took place in the nature of the questions presented to the courts. Previous to that time cases had for the most part been decided on the basis of the law of conspiracy. Since then applications for injunction have been the general rule. In regard to the law as determined by the courts up to that time, it may be said that in general the right to strike was limited to demands for better wages or improved conditions of labor. A series of struggles has come prominently before the courts within the last few years, in which has been involved the contention that a strike to accomplish purposes other than those above mentioned was also lawful. The main controversy has been to determine for what other purposes a strike might lawfully be conducted.

There have been three leading cases involving an interpretation of the law during this period. In order to compare them a brief review of each will be necessary. The first case was Curran *v.* Galen (1893–97). This has been cited frequently as an authority in connection with later cases involving a similar issue. The case itself was based upon the following facts: A laborers' association made an agreement with a Brewery Workingmen's Local Assembly of the Knights of Labor to the effect that all employees "shall be members of the Brewery Workingmen's Local Assembly No. ——, Knights of

Labor, and that no employee shall work for a longer period than four weeks without becoming a member." In accordance with this agreement the plaintiff in the case was discharged. He then brought action charging the defendants with conspiracy to injure him in his business and character and to prevent his obtaining employment; and furthermore demanded damages. The case was presented first to the special term of the supreme court, was carried to the appellate division, and from there to the court of appeals. The supreme court decided in favor of the plaintiff. They admitted that the defendants had a right to organize, but denied that they had a right to insist that others should join their organization, since this involved an interference with personal liberty to an extent not countenanced by law. The decision was further based on section 171 A of the penal code which makes it a misdemeanor for an employer to require as a condition of a person's entering or remaining in his employ that he shall not become a member of any labor organization. The spirit of this section was undoubtedly violated. This decision, then, sustained the plaintiff on two grounds; first, it "contravenes one of the fundamental principles of our free institutions," secondly, "it likewise violates the spirit if not the letter of a statute of this state." The court of appeals in reviewing this decision admits in the first place that it is "proper and praiseworthy" for members of society to unite to achieve that which they cannot achieve by themselves. Yet the social principle which justifies such organizations is departed from when they extend their operations so as to intend to accomplish injury to others. "If the purpose of an organization or combination of workingmen be to hamper, or to restrict, that freedom and . . . to coerce other workingmen to become members of the organization . . . under the penalty of the loss of their position . . . then that purpose seems clearly unlawful." The effectuation of such a purpose is held to conflict with "public policy." The case concludes as follows: "So far as the purpose appears . . . it is in effect a threat to keep persons from working at that particular trade and to procure their dismissal from employment."

The next case of importance was Davis *v.* United Engineers (1898). This case has also been cited very frequently. The case was brought in the appellate division on appeal. It was a case in which an engineer through the demands of an organization was deprived of employment in order that his place might be filled by a member of the organization. It was shown that the employer did not engage the plaintiff permanently, but was in the habit of sending for him when he could not secure a union man to do necessary work. As soon as a regular union man in good standing could be employed the plaintiff was immediately discharged. This was the fact upon which the decision hinged. The court held that "the plaintiff failed in establishing that his discharge was the result of a design on the part of the defendants, under any and all circumstances, to exclude him from making his livelihood." In this case again the right of laborers to organize in trade unions was admitted. It was further admitted that they have a right to refuse to work with persons who do not belong to their organization, and "whether they say it themselves or through their organized societies it makes no difference." Had it been shown in evidence that the plaintiff was a permanent employee, and that he was deprived of work "under any and all circumstances," the decision might have been in his favor.

The third important case involving this question, and the last one of prime importance decided by the courts of this state, was National Protective Association *v.* Cumming (1899–1902). This case was first tried before a special term of the supreme court, where an injunction was granted. It was carried to the appellate division, where the injunction was vacated. It was then appealed to the court of appeals. There the decision of the appellate division was sustained. It was a case between two rival labor organizations. One of the organizations held examinations for applicants. These examinations were tried by an applicant, who failed to pass them. Consequently he was not admitted to the union. He thereupon organized another union of the same trade and secured work. The first union then informed the employers that the members of the second union must be discharged or the business would be tied up. The discharges were accordingly made, and on this ground the matter was brought into the courts. The grounds on which the supreme court granted the injunction were those of Curran *v.* Galen, and the decision took particular pains to point out the difference between that case and Davis *v.* United Engineers, emphasizing especially the temporary character of the employment of the plaintiff in the latter case. The decision rendered by the court of appeals, reversing that of the lower court, was a long one, which entered fully into a discussion of the principles involved. Aside from the prevailing opinion, one other concurring opinion was written and one lengthy dissenting opinion. The opinion of the majority, delivered by the chief justice, ran as follows: First, the fact that an examination was required for admission into the defendant organization was significant. It was especially so in the present state of the law of liability of employers, for no adequate protection was then granted to an employee who was injured through the carelessness of a fellow-laborer. On this ground it seemed reasonable to hold that an organization which required each of its members to pass an examination showing efficiency was justified in refusing to work with a fellow-laborer who had failed to pass such an examination. At this point a statement in the dissenting opinion to the effect that an employee has no right to dictate to his employers how they shall carry on their business and whom they shall or shall not employ was questioned, on the ground that an employee has a right to require of an employer that he shall employ only persons with whom it is safe to work.

The decision next turned to broader considerations. It started from the same general principles that were stated in the dissenting opinion, but it applied them in a different way. This statement of common ground was as follows:

> It is not the duty of one man to work for another unless he has agreed to, and if he has so agreed, but for no fixed period, either may end the contract when he chooses. The one may work or refuse to work, at will, and the other may hire or discharge at will. . . . Whatever one man may do alone he may do in combination with others, provided they have no unlawful object in view. Mere numbers do not ordinarily affect the quality of the act. . . . They have the right to strike . . . . provided the object is not to gratify malice or to inflict injury upon others but to secure better terms of employment for themselves. A peaceable and orderly strike, not to harm others, but to improve their own condition, is not a violation of law.

After admitting the validity of this principle, the chief

justice went on to argue that one may refuse to work on any grounds deemed sufficient to himself. The employer has no right to demand a reason. If the reason is given, whatever it may be, it does not affect the right to stop work. This also applies to a body of men. It is their legal right to stop. Their reason cannot in law be demanded, but if they elect to state a reason, their right to stop is not cut off because the reason seems inadequate or selfish to the employer or to organized society. A desire to obtain higher wages, shorter hours or improved conditions does not include all the grounds which will justify strikes.

> The enumeration is illustrative rather than comprehensive, for the object of such an organization is to benefit all its members, and it is their right to strike, if need be, in order to secure any lawful benefit to the several members of the organization, as, for instance, to secure the re-employment of a member they regard as having been improperly discharged and to secure from an employer of a number of them employment for other members of their organization who may be out of employment, although the effect will be to cause the discharge of other employes who are not members.

Such an object cannot in the absence of evidence be interpreted as malice or desire to inflict injury upon others. On the question of motive, the opinion dissented from the proposition that a strike is lawful when its purpose is to help its members, and unlawful when merely to injure non-members. However, admitting the distinction in the refusal to work with non-members, the purpose must be assumed to be self-benefit unless positive proof is adduced to the contrary. It is only where the sole purpose is to do injury that the act becomes illegal. In threatening to strike, the defendants only threatened to do what they had a legal right to do. A threat is simply the giving of information, a simple notification of a determination to cease work. The foregoing line of reasoning was then applied to the facts of the particular case with the conclusion that the injunction should be vacated.

The minority opinion in this case was not so long, and its reasoning was more nearly along the line of the reasoning in previous cases, especially in Curran *v.* Galen. After laying down the first general principle which has been quoted above, the minority opinion held further: "They have no right, however, through the exercise of coercion to prevent others from working. When persuasion ends and pressure begins, the law is violated, for that is a trespass upon the rights of others, and is expressly forbidden by statute." The fact that force, threat or intimidation is unlawful is fully emphasized in this opinion. Moreover,

> a combination of workmen to secure a lawful benefit to themselves should be distinguished from one to injure other workmen in their trade. . . . Competition in the labor market is lawful, but a combination to shut workmen out of the market altogether is unlawful. One set of laborers, whether organized or not, has no right to drive another set out of business or prevent them from working for any person upon any terms satisfactory to themselves. . . . Depriving a mechanic of employment by unfair means is the same in principle as depriving a tradesman of a customer by unfair means, which has always been held a violation of law.

The object of the defendants in conducting this strike was held by the minority opinion to be evil, for it was not to compete for employment by fair means, but to exclude rivals from employment altogether by unfair means.

This was in violation of the principle that all men must have an equal chance to live by their own labor. In allowing one labor union to seize all the chances by compelling employers to accede to their demands, the motive was to force men who had learned a trade to abandon it. The answer to this line of reasoning has already been stated in the report of the prevailing opinion.

In summing up this case it may be stated again in the words of the court what the case actually decided. By a vote of four to three it held that

a labor union may refuse to permit its members to work with fellow-servants who are members of a rival organization, may notify the employer to that effect, and that a strike will be ordered unless such servants are discharged, where its action is based upon a proper motive, such as a purpose to secure only the employment of efficient and approved workmen or to secure an exclusive preference of employment to its members on their own terms and conditions; provided that no force is employed and no unlawful act is committed. If under such circumstances the employes objected to are discharged, neither they nor the organization of which they are members have a right to action against the union or its members.

In addition to these three leading cases may be noted one or two others of secondary importance. They show the attitude of the court toward the use of force. A case was decided by the appellate division after its decision in National Protective Association *v.* Cumming, but before that case reached the court of appeals. A printer sued to recover damages for a discharge caused through a strike by the union. He had been urged to join the Typographical Union, but as he was already a member of a Machinists' Union he refused. The employer had discharged him, as was shown upon evidence, in order to avoid a strike. The jury was instructed by the court after the trial to fix the amount of damages, and consequently damages were awarded. The appellate division reversed this decision on the same grounds that it had taken in the National Protective Association case.[1] This case later reached the court of appeals on grant of a new trial, and was decided (1904) in accordance with the National Protective Association case.

In another case the finding of the court was expressed in the following language:

> The case presented involves no more than refusal to work with members of the plaintiff association. . . . This does not amount to a conspiracy to prevent an employment under all circumstances, and in the absence of intimidation or of false statements as to the character of the laborers affected, the case discloses nothing unlawful in the attitude assumed by the defendants.[2]

The courts still insist, however, that all strikes shall be free from violence or force. In 1901 an injunction was granted against strikers. On appeal it was vacated because similar to the National Protective Association case. The appellate division, however, granted the injunction, stating that the National Protective Association case was no authority for resort to fraud, intimidation, force or threats. The union had been guilty of acts which were unlawful and unauthorized for the protection of any rights of which they were themselves possessed.[3] The same position was taken again in 1903.[4]

In the same year in a Monroe county case the court

[1] Wunch *v.* Shankland.

[2] Reform Club *v.* Laborers' Union.

[3] Beattie *v.* Callanan.

[4] Master Horseshoers' Protective Association *v.* Quinlivan.

made a distinction between lawful striking and picketing and unlawful war upon employers. The judge held to the law of the last-mentioned case, but found that the facts did not bring the case within that legal definition. Men may refuse to work with non-union men, but they may not compel a man to join an association by threatening to "utilize the entire power and enginery of the association to turn custom away from and promote hostility toward any one who dares to employ him as a punishment for giving him work." If they do this, they are "guilty of the crime of conspiracy to prevent another from filling his lawful occupation."

Closely related to cases involving the right to strike for any reason appearing to the striker as sufficient, is a line of decisions that define rather carefully the means that are lawful for strikers and their sympathizers to use in support of a strike. The most frequent of these auxiliary methods are picketing, boycotting, including the distribution of circulars urging the boycott, and the various means of deterring others from taking the strikers' places, such as arguments, inducements, threats, intimidation, coercion and the like.

Sleicher *v.* Grogan was a case in which employees had struck to secure higher wages and to unionize a foundry. After attempting unsuccessfully to keep the establishment running, the employers finally applied for an injunction to restrain the defendants from interfering with their rights. The court said:

The grounds on which this injunction is asked are briefly as follows: to prevent the defendants from interfering with the employes of the plaintiff; to prevent the defendants from loitering or lingering in or about the plaintiffs' premises with

[1] People *v.* McFarlin.

the view or purpose of interfering with or stopping the plaintiffs' business, and to prevent the defendants from interfering with the plaintiffs in the lawful prosecution of their trade or business.

The defendants were enjoined. An appeal was made, but did not come before a higher court until after the strike had been settled. The higher court, therefore, made no decision on the real case at issue, but vacated the injunction on the ground that it was no longer needed.

A case of wide general interest was the boycott of the New York *Sun* in 1899–1900. This boycott attended upon a strike against the decision of the management to open the printing rooms to non-union men. In the decision rendered in answer to the request for an injunction, the special term of the supreme court went further in the injunction than the appellate division would go in its review of the case. The judge in special term first reviewed the principle involved in Curran *v.* Galen, and in its application stated that

the defendants have in this case so conducted themselves as to come to some degree within this prohibition. It does not matter that their conduct has been self-contained and orderly; that they have resorted to no violence, nor even threatened any; that they have, in short, acted like intelligent capable men. . . . . Neither does it matter whether they have, as they claim, great and sufficient provocation for their strike.

Even assuming that the plaintiff was at fault and that defendants had just grounds for complaint, and further, that they have not carried on their contest in a blind spirit of resentment, but on the contrary, have directed their efforts in a rational manner, "notwithstanding all this, the fact remains that the law does not permit such warfare by such methods, whatever the provocation." The injunction was indeed a sweeping one. It enjoined the defendants from advising or requesting either by oral communication, by letters, or by printed circulars the advertising customers or persons who might become so to refrain from advertising in the paper; from resorting to any species of threats, intimidation, force or fraud to accomplish such purpose, or inducing other persons to do so; from preventing any person from selling the said newspapers; from picketing the establishment of the plaintiff for the purpose of intercepting its employees and inducing them to quit the employment of the plaintiff. A final paragraph of the injunction read as follows: "From in any other manner or by any other means interfering with the property, property rights or business of the plaintiff." This injunction proved too broad for the appellate division. In its revision it inserted in connection with each of the first three paragraphs the statement that the defendants were enjoined from doing any of the acts specified in the injunction, "in such manner as to express or imply a threat, intimidation, coercion, or force," and the final paragraph was stricken out entirely.

In a dispute arising over an issue involving the employment of only union men in a brewery, a strike was called, and the defendants applied for an injunction to prevent the strikers from picketing and using circulars to aid a boycott. The injunction was granted, and upon review by the appellate division was modified. The injunction was first granted enjoining the defendants from distributing certain circulars, or "any circulars whatever, referring to or reflecting upon the plaintiff, its business or its methods of business, or its conduct with relation to its employes or the goods manufactured, sold or delivered by it, or any part thereof," and furthermore from "congregating or assembling" near the entrances or in the vicinity of the plaintiff's place of business, or the place of business of any of the customers of the plaintiff, for the purpose of coercing such persons from doing business with the employers. After being reviewed by the appellate division, the order contained the following: "Nothing in this order contained shall be construed to prevent the defendants . . . from issuing and distributing the circular set forth in the complaint and injunction order . . . in a peaceable and orderly manner, unaccompanied by threats, violence or intimidation of any kind." Another difference between the two injunctions was that the second order expressly declared that it did not prevent the defendants from "accosting the plaintiff's employes or customers and the patrons of plaintiff's customers in a peaceable, orderly and decent manner for any purpose whatever."[1]

Another case of rather more importance than the one just referred to was Foster *v.* Retail Clerks' Protective Association. This decision made permanent an injunction against illegal picketing. While the court enjoined the union men from obstructing access to the store and interfering with travel in its neighborhood, it nevertheless recognized the right of the sympathizers of the strikers to carry on a peaceful boycott. The strikers were enjoined from entering the premises of the plaintiffs or interrupting their trade; from obstructing access to the store by physical means; from collecting in crowds in front of the store, obstructing travel on the street or sidewalk; from the use of threats with the intent of preventing customers from trading. "It should be remem-

[1] *Department of Labor Bulletin* (N. Y.), vol. iii, p. 145.

bered that to constitute intimidation it is not necessary that there should be any direct threat, still less any actual act of violence. It is enough if the mere attitude assumed by the defendants is intimidating." It developed in the evidence that the defendants were not employees of the plaintiff, nor even members of the union directly concerned. They were working men who were in sympathy with the efforts of the strikers. Their interest was held, therefore, to be "remote and uncertain."

Discussing the question as to whether picketing, apart from the motive, is in itself legal or illegal, the decision stated:

> There is nothing in a mere request not to deal which implies a threat to do an unlawful injury. Whether it does or does not depends on the circumstances in each case—upon exactly what is said and how it is said. Mere picketing, therefore, assuming that it is peaceful, assuming that there is no threat or intimidation, assuming that it is confined to simple persuasion, I do not regard in any sense as unlawful, whatever may be the motive of the picketers.

I may request my family not to trade with A or B for any reason that seems to me good. I have the same right to make the request of relatives or friends, and I have equal right to make the request of strangers by word of mouth or in writing. The place where I make the request is unimportant. "If I make it to one just entering A's store, the loss to A is more obvious, though no greater, than if I make it to an intending customer a mile away." The agreement to picket was then considered, and it was pointed out that the courts differed here also. Some have held that it is unlawful, since the combined efforts of several are more likely to be harmful than the act of one. Others have said that the reason is based upon the maxim that the injury done by one makes the loss so small that the law will not regard it. The whole theory, said the court, is erroneous. "Two or more persons may agree to do what each one of them may lawfully do," and it therefore seems that mere numbers co-operating in a picket does not make it illegal.

In 1902 the special term denied an injunction which was afterwards upon appeal granted.[1] The injunction was denied on the grounds that no violence was shown to have been done and that where violence is absent the rights of laborers are the same as the rights of other individuals. The decision was unanimously reversed on the ground that acts of violence and also threats or attempts to commit such acts were present, the affidavits in the case disclosing such evidence very clearly. This case is of further interest in that it specified certain acts which the court held to be acts of intimidation or violence. They were such acts as are well calculated

> to occasion fear in the minds of the plaintiffs' present employes, that a continuance in such employment would result in bodily harm. They included threats to "do" these workmen unless they join the strike; to "fight them man to man," to "beat every man that works in that shop;" to "fix" them so that they could never get another position in the United States; to lay for them and blow their heads off; to blow their brains out; to "lick" the men at night if they keep on working for the firm.

Actual violence is also detailed in the affidavits. One case, for example, consists "in the forcible seizure of the person of one of the workmen by the arm and pulling him across the street in an endeavor to prevent him from

[1] Herzog and Erb *v.* Fitzgerald.

entering the plaintiff's premises." These are only a few of the evidences selected from many cited in the case. The denials on the part of the defendants, so far as there were any, consisted in the reiteration of the general assertion that "at no time were any threats, force or intimidation used or attempted to be used," and that what was done was "in a peaceful and lawful way."

The latest important decision bearing on picketing and boycotting was rendered by the appellate division in the latter part of 1904.[1] The justice agreed with the former cases that have been cited upholding the right to picket and boycott, and based his reasoning on the line of argument in the National Protective Association case. The decision analyzed the question more fully than others have done, and pointed out the following distinctions: Picketing may mean the stationing of men "for observation;" or it may mean the stationing of men "to coerce or to threaten, or to intimidate . . . or in some other way to hamper" the business of the employer. In the former case the act is lawful; in the latter case "it may well be said to be unlawful." Similarly, in regard to the boycott a distinction was made. "Captain Boycott has added to our language a substantive and a verb. There is little if any question as to the meaning of the substantive, but there is no commonly accepted definition of the verb." Judge Cooley was quoted to the effect that

> It is a part of every man's civil right that he be left at liberty to refuse business relations with any person whomsoever whether the refusal rests upon reason or is the result of whim, caprice, prejudice or malice. With his reasons, neither the public nor third persons have any concern.

[1] Mills *v.* United States Printing Company.

Following this the justice gave his approval to the statement quoted from Bouvier: "A boycott is not unlawful unless attended with some act which in itself is illegal." The verb "to boycott," continued the justice, "does not necessarily signify that the doers employ violence, intimidation or other unlawful coercive means." On the other hand it may be correctly used to signify "the act of a combination in refusing to have business dealings with another" until he complies with their requirements. When such a combination is formed and held together by argument, persuasion, entreaty, or "by the 'touch of nature,'" and when it accomplishes its purpose "without violence or other unlawful means," but simply by abstention, "I think it cannot be said that 'to boycott' is to offend the law."

Here the development is completed so far as the courts have rendered decisions. Unless the decision last cited is overruled, there must be a careful distinction made as to the means used to enforce the picket and the boycott. Either act, *per se*, is not unlawful. But if unlawful acts attend the picket or the boycott, the unlawful acts themselves are punishable. The line of reasoning is so closely akin to National Protective Association *v.* Cumming that it seems altogether likely that it will stand. Only in case the decision of the court of appeals is reversed is the law likely to be changed in its attitude toward the picket and the boycott.

CHAPTER VIII

DEVELOPMENT OF THE LEGAL RIGHT TO ORGANIZE

An important part of the struggle by which labor organizations have gained their present standing has been the effort to secure the legal right to incorporate. This effort in its earlier stages showed very meager results. At first, as has been pointed out, the organizations were greatly hampered because they were held by the courts to be in restraint of trade and commerce. In 1870 the law was secured giving laborers the right to assemble and to co-operate in order to regulate wages. This was the first positive privilege granted to them. The next year through the efforts of the newly organized Workingmen's Assembly, a law was passed[1] providing for the incorporation of trade unions and societies of workingmen.[2]

This privilege was not without limitation, as unions were to be incorporated only under the act "for the incorporation of benevolent, charitable, scientific and missionary societies." The provisions and restrictions of that act were to apply in all respects. Some of the more important provisions were as follows: The act made the

[1] L., 1871, ch. 875.

[2] In 1792 an act was passed providing for the incorporation of a number of "Mechanicks and Tradesmen" of New York City into the "Society of Mechanicks and Tradesmen of the City of New York." The law authorized this one organization only, which was to exist for a limited number of years, and to be limited strictly to "charitable purposes."

organization a "body politic and corporate," capable of suing and being sued, of holding a limited amount of property "for the purposes of their incorporation and for no other purposes," and of making by-laws consistent with the laws of the state.[1] Thus the matter stood in 1871. A restriction in the law of 1848 had made it impossible for secret societies to be incorporated. The extension of the law in 1871 to include labor organizations indicated that progress had been made by these organizations toward the abandonment of that feature and that some of the prejudice prevailing against them had been thereby allayed.

In spite of the fact that the changes introduced by the law of 1871 were made primarily through the efforts of labor leaders, the latter were not satisfied. The act did not go far enough. Before the convention of 1887 the president of the Workingmen's Assembly stated his regret that "much to our discredit a law for the incorporation of trade unions as such is not yet upon the statute books," and that at present such unions could be incorporated legally only as "benevolent institutions requiring a benevolent clause." The struggle for the right of incorporation continued, but led to no immediate results. In 1887 the legislature passed the amendment to the penal code,[2] which made it a misdemeanor for an employer to require any employee not to join a labor union. This was a step forward but was still insufficient, especially as its provisions were not enforced. Moreover it was not what the leaders had in mind. With the dual cause for discontent—the ability to incorporate only as benevolent societies and the inability to enforce Section

[1] L., 1848, ch. 319.

[2] Sec. 171 A. l., 1887, ch. 688.

171 A of the Penal Code—the leaders continued the agitation. Every means at their command was used, but without the desired success. The question was a legal one involved in technicalities and the advocates of different bills found it difficult to win over the committees of the legislature. At the same time they were without means to employ legal aid. Year after year the question came up and as often came the report at the annual conventions, "measure failed." Yet the attitude of trade-unionists did not change and the words of the chairman of their committee continued to express the unanimous opinion, "The present law is an injustice to labor organizations."

It was not until 1895 that a point was gained. In that year was passed the membership-corporation law.[1] By its provisions a membership corporation could be created "for any lawful purpose." Labor unions were no longer classed as benevolent institutions before the law. The restrictions limiting them were the same as those limiting any other membership corporation.

In the next year another legal victory was won. By the benevolent-orders law[2] any number of trade unions were permitted to unite in forming a corporation to own a hall and collect a library for the use of such unions under the conditions provided in the law. Again in 1898 an advantage was secured. The unions were freed so far as the law could free them from a difficulty with which they had long been contending. A law was passed[3] making it a misdemeanor for any person to represent himself falsely as a member of any organization, or to present to

[1] L., 1895, ch. 559. Gen. Laws, ch. xliii, secs. 30, 31.

[2] L., 1896, ch. 377. Gen. Laws, ch. xliv, sec. 7.

[3] L., 1898, ch. 671.

any convention credentials so representing him, or in any other way to gain admission to a convention through false representations.

At this point ends the effort to secure special legal protection for the union as an organization. In the light of the persistent and protracted struggle for the right of legal incorporation, the number of unions that have availed themselves of the privilege is surprisingly small. The reasons for this fact are not immediately connected with this part of the subject. Yet the fact itself indicates the small practical value to the unions of this privilege. Efforts to strengthen the organizations of labor have gone on unabated, but the means used have not of late years been related directly to the legal side of the question. For this reason their consideration is not within the scope of the present chapter.

CHAPTER IX

JUDICIAL DECISIONS. LEGAL STATUS OF ORGANIZATION.

THE legal status of trade unions has not been determined by statute law alone. The decisions of the courts have had an important influence. The efficiency of an organization depends very largely upon the right of the union to conduct a strike. That legal right has already been discussed. Closely related to it are other matters that concern the organization very intimately, and upon which the courts of the state have rendered decisions. Among these are the right of a union to enforce its by-laws; the right of a member when expelled to secure reinstatement; the right of a union to execute its will through delegates, and the right to form a trade agreement with an employer for the purpose of excluding non-union laborers.

As has been stated, an early obstacle to be overcome was the view of the courts that these associations were combinations in restraint of trade and commerce, and were, therefore, conspiracies. This was the position taken in People *v.* Fisher in 1835. Master Stevedores' Association *v.* Walsh, in 1867, was the first case in which the court recognized that trade unions have a legitimate place in industry and that they are of undoubted advantage when they remain in that place. In this case it was stated specifically as the opinion of the court that an association if voluntary may enforce a by-law, if it is within its power to make such by-law, and may attach a penalty for the purpose of enforcing it. In 1888 a case arose which caused a division of the court on the question of the right of a union to enforce one of its by-laws.[1] In the charter of the defendant the object of the association was declared to be the cultivation of the art of music in all its branches; the promotion of good feeling and friendly intercourse among the members of the profession; and the relief of such of the members as should be unfortunate. A by-law of the union required every member to refuse to perform in any orchestra or band in which any person was engaged who was not a member of the union. The prevailing opinion took the view that the by-law was not at all designed to accomplish the declared objects of the union—either to promote good feeling or to relieve the unfortunate. Furthermore, the effect of the by-law was to create a closed corporation and to force each member of the profession to become a member also of the union. For these reasons the court declared that the by-law was not enforceable. The dissenting opinion took a different view. There was nothing in the letter of the law to prevent the validity of the rules of the union. The court should not, as a general rule, interfere with the contentions and quarrels of a voluntary association. Those who have grievances should resort first to the remedies for redress provided by the rules and regulations. There was thus presented a difference of opinion which, from the standpoint of legal development, was important. The former view, with its antipathy for closed corporations and its hostility toward any increase in membership, was the older. The latter with its growing sympathy for the organization of labor and the tendency to start the logical chain from

[1] Thomas *v.* Musical Mutual Protective Union.

the hypothesis of the individual right of the employee, was the newer. In it were stated more specifically the ideas that had been advanced in Master Stevedores' Association *v.* Walsh. It was not carried to the court of appeals and is of importance only as presenting clearly the two conflicting opinions. In 1900 the same general question came before the appellate division in a case in which a member had been expelled and had appealed to the courts for reinstatement.[1] In this instance the court held to the rule

> that the constitution and by-laws are the sole rule that governs the relations between the association and its members and that the courts cannot redress any action of the association in expelling or punishing a member when such action has been taken in accordance with the express provisions of the constitution and by-laws.

Here the view of the dissenting opinion in the case last noted was followed and was accepted as the view of the higher court.

A unique case was brought before the courts in 1901 in an attempt to convict a labor organizer as a public nuisance. The organizer was charged with circulating false statements, creating agitation, unrest and dissatisfaction and endeavoring to induce the laboring men to boycott their employers. The court found that the defendant was acting within the law, and after defining a public nuisance, decided that the definition did not include the case at bar.[2] An appeal was taken, but the case was not again brought to trial and was finally dismissed. No like attempt has since been made.

[1] Austin *v.* Dutcher.

[2] Chautauqua County Court, Oct. 12, 1901.

The expulsion of a member from a union because he was a member of the national guard was an episode that attracted much attention in the winter of 1902–3. So far as the legal side of the issue went nothing new was developed. The plaintiff was granted a temporary injunction in December, 1902, against his union, restraining it from enforcing a rule of the by-laws to the effect that a "militiaman, special police officer or deputy marshal in the employ of corporations or individuals during strikes, lockouts or other labor difficulties . . . shall be debarred from membership." In the following February the same justice vacated the injunction. The attempt was made to rest the claim of the plaintiff on the general principle of interference with public defense and the efficiency of the military power, and to make him the "champion of the sovereignty of the state." This the justice would not admit as pertaining to the case. It was found that there were doubts as to the plaintiff's standing in the organization. He had no full membership card, was receiving wages less than the scale set for a full member; in other words, in the opinion of the court, the full membership of the plaintiff was not established beyond a doubt. Obviously, the plaintiff could not "by injunction be reinstated if he never was instated." Since the facts did not show that the plaintiff had been expelled from full membership, the principles of the National Protective Association case were applied, and it was held that the members had a right to refuse to work with the plaintiff. Although the opinion did not state squarely the view of the court relative to the hostility of the unions to the state militia, yet the case aroused a sentiment throughout the state strong enough to secure the enactment of an amendment to the Penal Code. This amendment declared it a misdemeanor for trade unions to discriminate against members of the national guard because of such membership.[1] Just as the employers have finally succeeded in emasculating section 171 A of the Code, so it is not at all unlikely that the unions, whenever it may be to their interests, may succeed in practically nullifying the force of these two sections. This will be made easier as long as the principles of the National Protective Association case are followed. On the other hand, it is not at all unlikely that the sentiment in favor of a strong national guard may lead the courts to see a different principle involved and to fall back upon "public policy" as a ground on which to uphold the law. This would prevent the direct violation of the statute, yet it might not succeed in dealing successfully with the roundabout means of evasion that may easily be adopted. Especially is this the case if the court of appeals follows its own lead in refusing to consider motives. So long as the law stands, however, it places a definite limitation on the action of trade unions.

Another case bearing on the right to discharge a member came before the courts in 1902 and reached the court of appeals. The plaintiff had been fined by his union. Three months were given in which to pay the fine. The fine was not paid. Two months after the expiration of the period, the fine was offered and was rejected. According to the by-laws the union could only suspend until payment of fine. A *mandamus* was granted compelling the union to accept the fine and restore the plaintiff to membership. He then sued to recover damages for loss of employment during the period between the refusal of the fine and the issuing of the

[1] L., 1903, ch. 349. Penal Code, sec. 171 B, 171 C.

mandamus. The damages were awarded. The case was carried to the court of appeals where the decision was sustained.[1] There was no principle involved in the case other than that a union must live up to its by-laws, and, by inference, that it has no authority not expressed in its objects of incorporation and its rules made in accordance therewith. In another case a number of unionists refused to strike with their organization. They were expelled. They applied for *mandamus* to compel the union to reinstate them. The court decided the expulsion to be legal. The circumstances were peculiar, however, and were given special weight in determining the case. The union had just withdrawn from the Knights of Labor, and the by-laws of the old organization were inoperative. It was during the period in which the new by-laws were being formulated that the strike occurred, and consequently there were no by-laws in force. That condition, in the opinion of the justice, made the union "free to take any such action as it chose in entering on a strike" if consistent with its purposes of organization and if not unlawful. In accordance with National Protective Association *v*. Cumming, the strike was lawful, and it seemed to the justice

> that it was the duty of the plaintiff . . . . to obey its lawful resolutions, and that his refusal to obey the order to strike was sufficient ground for his expulsion. . . . . I cannot well see how the association could maintain its organization unless it punished its members who refuse to obey its lawful resolutions.[2]

Thus while the case was exceptional because of the con-

[1] 170 N. Y. mem. 43.

[2] *Department of Labor Bulletin* (N. Y.), vol. iv, p. 329.

dition of the by-laws, yet the court expressed its opinion that a union may discipline its members.

While from these cases it is quite evident that the courts will sustain the unions in the enforcement of their purposes of organization and the rules and regulations made in accordance with them, it also appears that when these rules and regulations are not followed properly in disciplining a member, the courts are inclined to look with legal disfavor upon the union violating them. The case of Corregan *v.* Hay is a case in point. The plaintiff was accused of making a speech detrimental to the interests of the organization in sufficient degree to afford cause for discipline. He was notified that charges would be preferred against him on a given date. Without "any formal charges having been presented to him or notice of the same in any manner given," the plaintiff was fined fifty dollars and suspended until the fine was paid. Thereupon the plaintiff demanded copies of the charges and of the evidence. Such demand was not regarded, but the plaintiff's employers were notified and the plaintiff was discharged. The court found "that the proceedings . . . and the suspension . . . were irregular. . . . No proper notice was given the plaintiff that the charges were to be preferred against him, and no opportunity was given him to defend himself." As another "conclusion of the law" the court found that "the plaintiff was bound to exhaust his remedies within the organization before appealing to this court for redress." The court concluded, however, that "under these circumstances it was unreasonable to require the plaintiff to prosecute his appeal within the organization as a prerequisite of bringing the action at bar, and that his failure to do so does not prevent his resorting to this court." If this opinion be taken as the law, it appears that the courts will interfere when the organization does not observe its rules and regulations in dealing with its members. At the same time, however, the opinion is expressed that as a general rule the means afforded by the organization for redress of grievances should first be exhausted.

There is yet a fourth point to consider, one of even greater importance than the foregoing. It pertains to the validity of those clauses of trade agreements by which organizations seek to secure to themselves exclusive employment in their trades. The cases involving this question have not been numerous, and such decisions as have been rendered do not bear directly on the general principle. It is not possible, therefore, to state clearly the law of the courts on the question. The practice of entering into a formal agreement instead of leaving the matter open to the constant possibility of a strike is new, and consequently there are no early cases bearing on the point. Curran *v.* Galen held that although the contract was drawn up for the purpose of avoiding disputes and conflicts, "such an intention cannot . . . legalize a plan of compelling workingmen not in affiliation with the organization to join it at the peril of being deprived of their employment and of the means of making a livelihood." This case, it will be remembered, was decided on the principle that trade unions could not use the means in question in their efforts to secure exclusive employment for their own members. The case came earlier than the National Protective Association case, at a time when the older ideas were still dominant. In 1902 there arose a case which dealt more directly with the question. Its object was to determine whether a union might secure an injunction to compel an employer to fulfill a contract to employ its members only. A second union had threatened to inaugurate a strike on all of the employer's work unless he dismissed the members of the first union. To avoid having his work tied up the employer discharged the members of the first union and gave their places to members of the second union. The court declined to allow an injunction in the case, holding that the union had the same remedy at law as a discharged employee, namely, an action for damages.[1] There were no cases cited in support of the plaintiff's contention, and when the counsel resorted to reasoning by analogy from other cases, such reasoning failed to convince the court of the propriety of interfering by injunction. In 1903 a case reached the appellate division to determine the validity of an agreement to arbitrate. Here again the case was decided on a point not bearing on the principle, as the claims of the plaintiffs were not based squarely on the agreement. It may be of interest to note the words of the court, though they are not to be taken as in any sense a final statement of law.

> It is not necessary at this time to decide how far this contract was in accord with public policy or how far it was binding upon the defendants. No consideration was expressed and it is apparent that the defendants were coerced into making this agreement . . . . practically as a condition of being permitted to continue their business. Under such circumstances it may be doubted whether the contract had any binding force on the defendants.[2]

There was an intimation in the case that public policy is a factor to be considered, and that should an instance be brought before that court it would be given considera- tion. Another intimation was that when no considera-

[1] Stone Cleaning and Pointing Union *v.* Russell.

[2] Eden *v.* Silberberg.

tion appears in the agreement, or when it is shown that one of the parties was coerced into making the agreement, it may not be allowed to stand at law as a contract. Within a year after the decision was written, such a case did come before the same court. It was a case of a joint agreement to secure the exclusive employment of members of the union. This case is among the most important that have arisen in this connection. It did not settle the question finally by any means, but it dealt more fully with it than any previous case. By the terms of the agreement the firm was to hire only members of the union, and even members were not to be hired without cards testifying to their good standing in the organization. "In view of these provisions . . . . it is plain," said the justice, "that the covenant . . . . is an engagement on the part of the firm to discharge" persons upon receipt of notice that the card is withdrawn. "The combination disclosed is accordingly one the purpose of which is to hamper and restrict freedom of employment . . . . and to coerce all workingmen within the field of its operations to become and to remain members of the contracting organization." Applying the principles of Curran *v.* Galen, the justice said: "Although the question may not be altogether free from doubt, I think the spirit and the reasoning [of that case] condemns this contract as illegal." The court accordingly decided that the agreement was contrary to public policy, three justices concurring. In a dissenting opinion the other two justices united in accepting the reasoning that an agreement might hold good even though it was restrictive, provided it was clearly evident that the purpose was

to secure the best service in the performance of the work which he desires to have done, although the effect of the agreement is in some respects detrimental to others, as, for example, to those who are not admitted to his service because they do not belong to an organization of working-men whom he deems best fitted to perform the labor which he desires performed.

It was not pleaded that the agreement was to injure others or to hamper their freedom.

In my opinion a contract having the lawful purpose of benefiting the parties thereto by procuring for the employer the most capable workmen, and not involving the exercise of any physical force or restraint or violence is not invalidated because of the possibility or probability that its operation may have a detrimental effect upon the interests of others.

Here again the justices held conflicting opinions. The opinion of the majority was purposely expressed so as not to be final. The opinion of the minority was of course not law in any event, but it also was expressed in an informal way which indicates a doubt as to its finality.[1] It was the same difference of opinion once more that has already been noted; turning on the question of force, motives and individual rights. To show how real this uncertainty is, it is only necessary to point out that soon after the decision just referred to was rendered, the same court held another trade agreement to be legal.[2] This was an agreement to employ only members of certain unions after a fixed date, it being provided that all non-union men then employed in the shop were to be eligible to membership. The justice who wrote the dissenting opinion in the previous case wrote the prevailing opinion in this case. The opinion was unanimously affirmed. The principles of National Protective Association *v.* Cumming prevailed, the court refusing to interfere, since

[1] Jacobs *v.* Cohen. [2] Mills *v.* United States Printing Company.

an employer could refuse to employ any one on any grounds that were satisfactory to himself.

So far, then, as these cases go, the question is still undecided. Curran *v.* Galen and National Protective Association *v.* Cumming still furnish two lines of reasoning, either one of which may be made applicable to a trade agreement that has for its object the exclusive employment of any group of men. The latter, when applied without modification, affirms unqualifiedly the legality of such agreements. The former, when similarly applied, leads to a restriction and even to a declaration that such agreements are illegal. The declaration of illegality can be maintained, as it seems, only on the ground that such an agreement is contrary to public policy. This was the interpretation in Curran *v.* Galen. It has been held by the court of appeals[1] that "parties cannot make a binding contract in violation of law or of public policy." If the court can be convinced that an agreement to secure exclusive employment is clearly contrary to public policy, there is the authority above cited for declaring that contract void. There is the further possibility of showing the contract to be the result of coercion. In that case it would come within the last citation, being a contract in violation of law.

These few cases show that it was the opinion at the outset that such a contract should never be subject to interference through an injunction. Then a contract was held by a divided court to be illegal. Later, by an undivided court one was held to be legal. The question has not reached the court of appeals. The illegality rests on the interpretation of public policy. This is a proposition that can be applied only to particular cases as they arise and no general principle is to be formulated.

[1] Sternaman *v.* Met. Life Ins. Co., 170 N. Y., 13.

CHAPTER X

DISCUSSION OF CASES

THE most cursory review of the decisions during the past fifty years cannot fail to reveal the constantly increasing variety of cases that are brought before the courts. Even during the last decade both the number and variety are strikingly large. Non-union men have sought injunctions against employers and against union men. Unions have moved against rival organizations. Unions have sought to enjoin employers, and employers to enjoin unions. Injunctions have been asked against all phases of the boycott, picketing, and use of circulars. An organizer has been prosecuted as a public nuisance. Citizens have appealed to prevent the monopolization of public work by union labor. Taxpayers have sought *mandamus* to compel public officials to enforce the provisions of the labor law. Union men have sought the aid of courts to secure reinstatement into unions from which they have been discharged. Such are some of the issues that the courts have been called upon to settle, and from them has been gradually developed a body of court-made law which is an important part of the social legislation of the state.

Several reasons exist which tend to make the principles less clear than they might otherwise be, yet from the nature of our court system the difficulty cannot be altogether avoided. Minor points are often given a deciding influence in a case, so that the case is not decided on any broad principle. This is doubtless necessary. Often again an apparent difference in principle in two cases proves to be only a difference in the value ascribed to some point of evidence or in the circumstances. As, for example, according to Foster *v.* Retail Clerks' Protective Association a request not to deal with a merchant does or does not imply a threat depending "on the circumstances of each case—upon exactly what is said and how it is said." From such cases principles that are applicable to action are not easily deduced since a slight difference in circumstances would prevent a case from being covered by the decision.

The fact that many decisions are reversed, though not so serious an obstacle in the way of one seeking to formulate the principles of the law as developed by the courts, constitutes an element of uncertainty. Cases are on record where the decision of the court of first trial has been reversed by an appellate court and the court of last resort has reversed the appellate court decision, sustaining the first opinion. Sometimes courts of first trial are sustained and at other times not. The dissenting opinion will sometimes quote in support of its position statements made in decisions that have been reversed by higher courts. In one case a strike against non-union men was decided in favor of the plaintiff, one leading case being cited as authority, and the decision was afterwards reversed on the ground that the case cited did not apply, but that another leading case was the proper authority. In general it may be said that the lower courts will follow the older principles; while the newer principles, keeping pace with the social changes, will be announced first by the higher courts. In injunctions also the lower courts have been more willing to grant sweeping restrictions. These have often been modified materially by courts of appeal.

Still further it is to be noted that the courts hold strictly to the legal phases of the question and do not pronounce upon the broader moral phases except incidentally. They have suggested that there is a broader moral side to the contention and have occasionally hinted that it should have weight, yet after a case has once come into court, they insist that only legal considerations shall have weight. The following quotation is a case in point:

> While I may not commend the course at times pursued by —— —— to secure to the members of the defendant society preference of employment, ... I do not discover that those acts were unlawful or were committed in the accomplishment of an unlawful purpose. . . . If the members were temporarily deprived of occupation by reason of lawful business rivalry, no relief can be had.[1]

This insistence on the doctrine that cases once in court must be settled on strictly legal principles is to be commended. It is true that many considerations not strictly legal should have weight in effecting an adjustment between laborers and their employers. The importance of this is pointed out more fully in another place. But when the entire authority of the state is to be called in to enforce an adjustment, force should be used only in support of such moral ideas as have been adopted by the members of that state as applicable to that society. Those moral standards or ideas which have not yet been given a legal force should not be directly appealed to in court action.

[1] Reform Club of Masons and Laborers *v.* Laborers' Union Protective Society.

At times, however, the courts have turned aside from the main point to give advice or point a moral lesson. Sinsheimer *v.* United Garment Workers was a case where the employers were seeking to enjoin laborers from prosecuting a strike to raise wages. The evidence showed that the employers had themselves formed an association to unite in reducing wages. The same efforts were being made by both sides and nothing illegal was being done by either side. The court pointed out that "it is a familiar principle in equity that the plaintiff must come into court with clean hands." In another case may be found the following:

> These plaintiffs seem to have brought on the trouble by ostentatiously and needlessly posting in their factory a notice that they will not recognize the union. Wiser employers have learned that it is a convenient and useful thing to recognize labor unions and to deal with them. The motion is denied but all the persons concerned should be careful to break no law.

Here the employers were lectured. In People *v.* Wilzig the laborers received the admonition: "Let me give a single word of counsel to those who are combining in trades unions and similar associations of laboring men. Before they appoint an executive committee or even a finance committee, let them appoint a committee on the law."

Passing beyond these relatively minor considerations, an analysis of the cases reveals some important facts in connection with the development of principles. A very important change has taken place in the application of conspiracy to strikes. As is shown by the review of early cases all strikes were at first unlawful, because they were conspiracies. Although the New York Cordwainers' case, in 1809, did not positively assert that an agreement not to work was a conspiracy, yet it did hold that a strike to force the agreement on the employers was a conspiracy. Conspiracy was defined in the time-honored way, "a combination to do an unlawful act or a lawful act by unlawful means." How this definition could have held the position it has, is difficult to understand; for it seems clear that to do a lawful act by *unlawful means* is simply to do an unlawful act. This would render the person liable to prosecution for the unlawful act, irrespective of whether that act is a means, or whether it is an end in itself. But such a definition seemed necessary since in no other way could the agreement be made the "gist of the crime." Thus, it was necessary to assume that an agreement was unlawful in order to establish its unlawfulness in court. The idea was a part of the general more or less hazy notion of conspiracy, which seems to have been the most indefinite and confused part of the law. Through the several important cases that have been before the courts since 1809 this idea has been materially changed. The agreement not to work except for certain wages was shown never to have been held unlawful either in English or American law. From this has developed the present interpretation. In People *v.* Trequier, when it was established that "on one occasion they all together objected to work," this organized objection was held to be a conspiracy. The first positive step forward was in the Stevedores' Association case, which made positive the implication of People *v.* Fisher that an agreement in itself was legal. Later came a distinction between an agreement among workmen not to work and an agreement to compel other journeymen to refuse to work. The former was held to be lawful, while the latter was unlawful. This distinction was pronounced to be a "step toward reason and justice." As late as 1867 an association to quit the service of an employer who employed journeymen below certain fixed rates was conspiracy. With the statute of 1870 came a further step forward. Yet as late as 1888 a strict-construction view of the law was taken. A strike if peaceful or for better wages or improved conditions of labor was legal; but when there was no relation direct or indirect between the rate of wages or the conditions of labor and the strike, the strike was illegal. Since that date the courts have been emphasizing the rights of individuals, and have come to the position that a strike for any purpose is legal, and that no interference need be expected from the courts unless individual or property rights are interfered with; then the courts will take account of the lawlessness, but not of the strike. Thus the old definition of conspiracy has found its correct interpretation. The unlawful means are treated as any other unlawful acts, and conspiracy has lost its force as a means for combating the movements of organized labor.

While the courts have been very clear in stating that an organization has a right to cease work in a group for any reason whatever, it has been equally clear in insisting that all forms of force, coercion, violence, threats or intimidation must be absent from the strike. As early as 1886 it was held that workmen could urge others not to work if they did not employ violence, threats or intimidation. It is difficult to analyze the cases of the earlier period for the reason that the reports are not so full, and for the further reason that the courts did not attempt so clear a distinction between the strike itself and the use of force or violence to enforce it. Conspiracy was often found when it is not clear whether the strike or the violence was the more important reason for the finding. In 1867 "any attempt by force, threat, intimidation or other coercive means to control a man" was held to be conspiracy when undertaken by a combination. The distinction has been growing constantly clearer. In 1894 one of the justices stated: "I know of no law which prevents combination . . . as long as the acts of such associates do not infringe upon the provisions of the law."[1] In 1901 an injunction granted by a lower court was held to be too sweeping, and was modified so as not to cover the doing of the acts in a "peaceable and orderly manner unaccompanied by threats, violence or intimidation." On the other hand an injunction was refused a year later by a lower court, and on appeal the higher court granted the injunction restraining especially from "commission of acts of violence and also from threats or attempts to commit such acts." It thus has come to be the settled opinion of the courts that in the absence of force, coercion, violence, threats or intimidation, strikes are not unlawful acts. But where persuasion ends and pressure begins, in efforts to induce laborers to leave work in support of a strike, at that point begins violation of law.

While such is clearly the opinion of the courts, yet it cannot be said to settle the cases finally. The particular acts of strikers and their sympathizers may come within the definition of the terms or they may not. This is a point for the courts to determine in each particular case. No comprehensive definitions of the terms have been formulated. A case in 1902 held that "to constitute intimidation it is not necessary that there should be any direct threat, still less any act of violence. It is enough if the mere attitude assumed by the defendants is intimidating."[2] In 1891 "the obtaining of money from an-

[1] Sinsheimer *v.* United Garment Workers.

[2] Foster *v.* Retail Clerks' Protective Association.

other with his consent induced by a threat that his workmen who had been on strike would not return to work unless the money was paid"[1] did not come within the idea of lawlessness held by the court.

As stated above, the law of conspiracy is seldom, if ever, invoked to control strikers. Its place is taken by the injunction. In granting injunctions the courts follow the same idea as to rights and as to force as are applied under other circumstances. Injunctions are generally not granted except to prevent force, damage or irreparable infringement upon some right.

Another important development in these decisions is the importance attached to the motives of workmen. The difference was early pointed out when, in 1806, it was said that combinations to raise wages may be considered from a twofold point of view: "one is to benefit themselves; the other is to injure those who do not join their society." Both were at that time unlawful. Later a distinction was made. If the motive was to improve the condition of the laborer, it was legal; if it was to preserve unions and displace non-union men, it was illegal. This distinction resulted very directly from the legislation of 1870, which made it legal to unite for certain purposes. The next step was to hold the refusal to work with non-union men to be self-interest and not malice, and, therefore, lawful. The burden of proof was next placed on those endeavoring to prove an unlawful motive, and a strike to secure employment to members could not in the absence of direct evidence be interpreted as malice or a desire to inflict injury. This was next extended to cover all cases of strikes. The distinction was then clearly made between a combination to secure lawful

[1] People *v.* Barondess.

benefit and one to injure other workmen; if not to "gratify malice or inflict injury" the strike is lawful, and it is only when such malice is positively proven that it may be held to be the guiding motive. The next position could only be that a strike was illegal only where the sole purpose was proven to be the doing of injury. From this the last effort to distinguish between motives passed away, and the courts look only at the acts. "I am not willing to hold that a request not to patronize a certain dealer may be legal if made by a person in one state of mind, or holding one relation to him, and illegal in another."[1] National Protective Association *v.* Cumming dissented entirely from the opinion that the legality of a strike depends on motive—lawful when the purpose is to help members, and unlawful when merely to injure non-members. It took the unqualified position that a man may stop work for any reason that seems good to him, and that an organization of men may do the same.

If the courts can succeed in maintaining the position that motives for acts are not to be considered, the doctrine will greatly simplify the entire question, for motives are exceedingly complex, and few acts are ever done from a single motive. The problem of ascertaining what the dominant motive is in any case is at best one uncertain of correct results. Futhermore, it may be urged with some force that so far as possible it should be the province of the courts to pass upon acts and not upon the reasons which prompt them.

Rising in importance above any of the points that have thus far been referred to is the question of the adjustment of "individual rights" and "social rights." In the maintenance of individual rights the courts have been

[1] Foster *v.* Retail Clerks' Protective Association.

very positive in the more recent decisions, though the same can not be said of their earlier decisions. At first their view was highly colored by the prevailing notion that in some way the equality between man and man did not apply when one man was an employer and the other his employee. The notion of the status of the laborer entertained in England in the previous century and brought to this country in spite of the declarations of Fourth-of-July principles had an influence largely unconscious on the minds of the judges during the first decade of the nineteenth century. The terms journeyman, master-workman and others having so much of the flavor of the previous century still retained the implied meaning of the social conditions in which they originated. This influence did not continue long, but it may be found in the earlier cases. It was followed by an application of the ideas of absolute equality and absolute individual liberty—the notion that pervaded all the thought of the major part of the nineteenth century. It was the application of this principle that led the courts to advance along the lines that have been pointed out above. Conspiracy could not live in an atmosphere of individual liberty; only when force was used could the acts of strikers be curbed in such an atmosphere; and finally, it was this atmosphere that first caused an investigation into motives and a distinction between motives, and at last a refusal to consider them as having any weight. But now that these results have been acccomplished, it is beginning faintly to appear that the principle must be modified. While no definite step has been taken, yet it is clear that some such step must be taken in the near future.

Look at some of the statements in court decisions and see how impossible it is to reconcile them on the basis of individual liberty. The employer has the absolute right to employ or refuse to employ whom he pleases. The employee has the absolute right to work or to refuse to work for whom he pleases. It must follow that an employer can refuse to employ members of any organization; that an employee can refuse to work with members of any rival organization; an employer can insist on employing one organization only; and an employee can refuse to work unless with his organization only. These statements may all be found more than once in court decisions and have the authority of the highest courts of the state. It requires no more than the statement to make clear the inconsistency. A decision that a strike is lawful or that it is unlawful will follow depending on which of the two contrary hypotheses is taken to start with. As has been said, in the early cases the rights of man usually rested with the employer. Starting from this premise, the employer could employ whom he chose and a combined refusal to work with any one whom an employer chose to employ was conspiracy. Curran *v.* Galen started with the same premise (though the old idea that the workman had no rights had disappeared) and reached the conclusion that an organization could not refuse to work with members of another organization if the employer chose to employ them. When, on the other hand, the course of reasoning was started from the premise of the right of the employee as an individual, no other conclusion could possibly be reached than that the employee could refuse to work whenever he saw fit. This dilemma has forced the courts to the conclusion that the law in its present development cannot take account of the essential point, and therefore it declares the absolute right of every one to follow his own wishes and then keeps order by enjoining all parties from unlawful acts.

In the National Protective Association case, the dissenting opinion started with the same general principle with which the prevailing opinion began. The one emphasized the view that the right of one side would be trespassed upon if the case were decided one way and comes to one conclusion. The other concluded that the rights of the other side would be invaded if the case were decided the other way, and comes to the opposite conclusion. To strengthen the position of the dissenting opinion, the use of force was emphasized and made to appear important. In Curran *v.* Galen it was emphasized that one has a perfect right to join an organization, but has no right to insist that others should do so. To deprive one of labor because he refuses to join an organization is an infringement of personal liberty. Yet according to the opposite line of reasoning it might just as well have been argued that one may stop work for any reason he chooses, and if by so doing he can make it appear to the interest of his employer to discharge certain men, he is acting within the scope of his own personal liberty, and therefore is not trespassing upon the personal liberty of another. In another place it was held that one set of laborers had no right to drive another set out of their employment. On the contrary, it might have been held that one set may refuse to work until the employer does discharge the rivals. In that case they are driven out of employment. In only one or two cases does there appear an effort to solve this enigma. "The right of employer and employe is reciprocal" but "once that right is destroyed, personal liberty is destroyed and chaos reigns." A more definite limitation on the right of the employer is pointed out by the chief justice in National Protective Association *v.* Cumming. In cases of dangerous employment, especially under the existing status of the liability of employers, an employee has the right "to dictate to employers how they shall carry on their business" and "whom they shall or shall not employ" in order to secure safe conditions of labor.

The possibility of appealing to the law of conspiracy because of the combination has been eliminated in a very positive way. Again and again has it been emphasized that the freedom of organization to secure what an individual may lawfully strive for is guaranteed. If one has this right (to work or not as he chooses) he does not lose it by acting with others. If one individual does not possess the right to dictate for what pay another shall work, then no number of individuals can possess such a right. Two or more persons may agree to do what each of them may lawfully do. It follows, then, that employers and employees alike have the right to combine to accomplish ends that are in themselves lawful. The struggle is transferred from the field of individual rivalry to that of organized rivalry. The right of the laborer to organize is at last fully admitted both by statute law and by the courts. Yet there is still the insistence on individual liberty in the organizations. The principle of individual rights still holds. Curran *v.* Galen admitted that co-operation is not against any public policy and that for the proper purposes it has the sanction of law. It is "proper and praiseworthy," and

> falls within that general view of society which perceives an underlying law that men should unite to achieve that which each by himself cannot achieve, or can achieve less readily. But the social principle which justifies such organizations is departed from when they are so extended in their operation as either to intend or accomplish injury to others.

This is immediately followed by the reiteration of the rights of the individual and the importance of their protection, and the organization idea is soon lost. These points which affect somewhat the conflicting principles that have been pointed out are not of sufficient importance to modify them materially. In conclusion it may be said, then, that the courts stand upon this ground: the maintenance of the rights of each party regardless of the conflict that arises; and whenever such conflict does come the courts can only insist on the observance of all rights as far as possible, and insist further that peace shall be maintained and all laws observed.

The discussion of economic principles has been seldom entered upon by the courts and never in any comprehensive way. The decisions are based almost entirely on legal principles. Until the passage of the law defining conspiracy so as to include injury to trade or commerce, the only economic principles were those involved in the older social ideas of the relation of the laborer to his work and to his employer. Only one prominent case came before the courts to be decided squarely on the issue of injury to trade or commerce. That case was People *v.* Fisher, in 1835. It has been fully summarized[1] and needs little comment to point out the peculiar mixture of sense and nonsense contained in its lines. As it was in the day when competition was a popular catchword and supply and demand stood for an idea too hazy to be defined outside of the books of the "dismal science," it is but natural that these expressions should be found in the discussion, and that their meaning should not be at all clear. It is first stated that the raising of wages and a conspiracy for that purpose are matters of public concern.

[1] *Supra*, p. 62, *et seq.*

Later comes this remarkable sentence: "Whatever disputes may exist among political economists upon the point, I think there can be no doubt in a legal sense but what the wages of labor compose a material portion of the value of manufactured articles." Following this is the reasoning by which it is shown that the one town suffers, and that that is all that is necessary to bring the case within the statutes. "It is important to the best interests of society that the price of labor be left to regulate itself, or rather be limited by the demand for it." Accordingly it would follow from the former that competition is not to be free in labor, and from the latter that the price of labor is to be free to regulate itself "or rather" to be regulated by the employer. Here also appears the notion that the employer should be the factor of prime importance, since demand is to be active while nothing is said of supply. Yet another factor in fixing wages is described in the following words: "Without any officious or improper interference on the subject, the price of labor or the wages of mechanics will be regulated by the demand for the manufactured article or the value of that which is paid for it." At the same time the writer holds to the well-established maxim that competition is the life of trade, and further that combinations

> to enhance or reduce the prices of labor or of any article of trade or commerce are injurious. They may be oppressive by compelling the public to give more for an article . . . . than it is worth, or, on the other hand, of compelling the labor of the mechanic for less than its value.

The discussion is of little economic significance; it simply embodies some of the popular phrases of the day, while the real decision hinges upon the presence of conspiracy to accomplish the objects desired.

The next case that touched upon the economic phase of the problem was Master Stevedores' Association *v.* Walsh, in 1867. There had been an apprehension that if organizations of workmen were allowed to continue unchecked by the law they would become a menace by creating a monopoly of labor, and that employers would be placed wholly at the mercy of workmen with power to exact extravagant sums. This apprehension the justice holds to be "altogether an imaginary one." English legislation on the subject of wages and trade unions shows that

it is neither in the power of prohibitory laws nor of artificial combinations to control arbitrarily the price of labor and that no combination can devise any general regulation or scheme that will bring to the same level the skillful and incompetent, the diligent and the idle. All such matters regulate themselves. If labor is in demand, the rate of compensation will be enhanced in proportion, and if it is not, no combination among workmen can prevent the falling of prices.

Agreements among such organizations are "effectual only when their demands are just and reasonable, and when they attempt anything more they not only fail of their object, but are themselves the chief sufferers." When their demands are unreasonable, "by the natural law of demand and supply others will come in and take their places." Then in a more positive way the advantages of organization are pointed out, and for the time in which it was written the reasoning is certainly comprehensive. Much of it is as sound to-day as it was then, and is well worth careful study. The conclusion is that

it is better for the law to leave such matters to the action of the parties interested—to leave master workmen or jour-

> neymen free to form what associations they please in relation to the rate of compensation so long as they are voluntary. They mutually act upon each other.

Still the voluntary element is insisted upon, and no intimidation or coercion can be allowed.

The economic view of People *v.* Fisher was held in a case as late as 1888. A strike had been entered upon to secure the discharge of some co-employees. The court held to the strict construction of the statute to the effect that strikes were legal only when there was a direct relation between wages and the strike. If no such relation existed the strike was a conspiracy. It "involves a diminishing of the quantity of productive labor," and consequently it is "an injury to the community and an act injurious to trade."[1]

A more important matter than this within the field of economics is the attitude toward competition and monopoly as a phase of strikes. This is dealt with more fully in National Protective Association *v.* Cumming than in any other case coming within this review. It will be recalled as a case where one organization undertook to drive a rival organization from the field and to secure the employment to its own members. As to the economic phase of the question involved, the two opinions took opposite positions. The dissenting opinion held that it was an act which was in effect the securing of monopoly. The labor of the workman is his property.

> Competition in the labor market is lawful, but a combination to shut workmen out of the market altogether is unlawful. One set of laborers has no right to drive another set out of

[1] People *ex rel.* Gill *v.* Smith.

business or prevent them from working for any person upon any terms satisfactory to themselves.

This case was held to be a case of coercion, and therefore it was a combination to restrain the "free pursuit . . . of any lawful business in order to create and maintain a monopoly." Such a combination is by the laws of the state illegal. "The defendants could not drive the plaintiff's members from the labor market absolutely and the plaintiff could not drive the defendants' members therefrom." Public policy requires that the wages of labor should be regulated by the laws of competition and of supply and demand, the same as the sale of food or clothing. On the other hand, the majority opinion views the matter in a different light. "Regarded . . . as a mere struggle for exclusive preference of employment on their own terms and conditions, . . . how can it be said to be within the condemnation of the law or of any statute when there was no force employed nor any unlawful act committed?" Within the principle of competition, "if the motive be to destroy another's business in order to secure business for yourself, the motive is good." A man has an undoubted right to start a store and to sell at such reduced prices as to drive out competitors, after which he regains his losses. "Such has been the law for centuries." "The reason, of course, is that the doctrine has generally been accepted that free competition is worth more to society than it costs, and that on this ground the infliction of damage is privileged." So an organization undertakes to drive out its rivals. They are willing to bear the expense of a strike to accomplish this result if necessary, and they inform the employer to that effect. In this they are within the law, just as a storekeeper would be if, instead of hiding his purpose, he openly declared to his rivals that he intended to drive them out of business in order that he might later profit thereby. Thus it appears that competition is admitted, but the struggle should not go to the extent of securing monopoly. On the other hand, competition is to be preserved even when pursued to its logical consequences, always provided that the laws are observed. The courts are unsettled on the question, but the final prevailing decision of the highest court (four to three) opens the way for monopoly of labor. As the decision was by such a narrow majority, it is by no means to be taken as a settled opinion.[1] The reasoning of the dissenting opinion is strong, and any one of the members of the majority has but to change his mind and competition again will rise above monopoly, or, in other words, a limit more rigid than simply "unlawful acts" will be put on what an organization may do in its attempt to crush rivals. It appears, then, that while some steps have been taken toward the legal solution of the question of a labor monopoly resulting from successful competition, the final word has by no means been spoken. While the decision stands as law, it stands on too uncertain a foundation to be considered permanent. Furthermore, the developments in the movement of labor monopoly are too new to have been finally passed upon by the courts.

In the light of the decisions of the courts relating to the individual rights of employers and employees, it is pertinent to ask: Has Section 171 A of the Penal Code lost its force? This section was added in 1887, and provided that an employer should not "coerce or compel" an employee "to enter into an agreement either written

[1] The court of appeals has since given a unanimous decision in a later case upholding the majority opinion in this case. No opinion was written. Wunch *v*. Shankland (1904).

or verbal" not to join a labor organization as a condition of employment. Section 653 defines coercion as (1) using violence or inflicting injury or threatening such violence or injury; (2) depriving a person of tools or clothing, or (3) attempting intimidation by threats or force. An employer, as has been shown, can employ or refuse to employ any one for any reason. An organization may strike to secure the employment of its members even if others are discharged to make room for them.

Employers may legally refuse to employ men who belong or who do not belong to a particular organization, and one who merely induces an employer to act accordingly is not guilty of a wrongful or illegal act. In other words, to get a certain number of men to employ a certain class of men is not illegal; not wrongful on the part of either the employer or those who induce the employer to enter into such an agreement.[1]

If an employer has this scope of action legally, it certainly is not necessary to resort to acts which would come within the definition of coercion, as quoted above, in order to induce an employee either to join or not to join an organization as he may desire. He can simply discharge a person without reason—an act which comes within his individual right. He can then re-employ him for any reason or no reason at all when that employee withdraws from the union. In addition to this phase of the question, there is evidence that in fact the law has remained practically a dead letter. In 1888 the Workingmen's Assembly adopted a resolution naming cases of firms who had discharged employees "on the sole charge of their connection with organized labor." In 1892 the

[1] Reform Club of Masons and Plasterers *v.* Laborers' Union Protective Society.

Commissioner of Labor stated in his annual report[1] that "the provision of 1887 has remained a dead letter. Employers have continued to coerce employes into withdrawing from unions. . . . All attempts to secure the punishment of employers thus most obviously guilty of a misdemeanor have proved fruitless."

It is evident that this law accomplishes practically nothing in aiding the organizations to maintain their position. It leaves the whole question open to rivalry between employer and employee, with the possible difference that it forces the employer to accomplish his ends in a more indirect way—using diplomacy instead of the harsher means forbidden by the law.

[1] Part i, p. 37.

CHAPTER XI

CONCLUSION

THE preceding chapters have described the growth of trade unions and the development of the laws in which their rights and duties are defined. It must be evident to every reader how steady has been that development and how considerable have been the gains made in the direction of freedom of action for the representatives of organized labor. The path has certainly not been one of roses for those labor leaders who have been active in securing these results. Often the progress has been too slow to satisfy their impetuosity. Often the signs of progress have been so obscure as to be almost undiscernible except by those possessed of peculiar insight. Such halting progress was, however, inevitable, since there must needs accompany these changes a slow development in public opinion or a gradual transition in social and economic conditions. It is perfectly evident that the courts have reflected with considerable accuracy those social and economic ideals which have prevailed at different times. Wherever dissatisfaction has arisen it has generally been due to the fact that new ideals were yet in process of formation; that they had not yet become sufficiently general to warrant the court in putting the stamp of legality upon them. This attitude of conservatism the courts have maintained in spite of the criticism freely offered by the more zealous and impatient champions of the newer ideals.

One of the most important reasons for the steady development in the court decisions lies in the fact that a distinction is now possible which was impossible in earlier times. Formerly the intense feeling engendered by a strike almost inevitably led to a riot, destruction of property and other unlawful acts. So intimately connected were such acts with the strike itself that they were an inseparable part of the definition of the word. Even to-day something of the old idea remains, for to many people the term strike is synonymous with law-brcaking. With the advent of strong and clear-sighted leaders it began to appear that some strikes at least could be conducted with little or no lawlessness. This has been of great benefit in enabling the courts to insist on the distinction in legal thought between a strike as a concerted refusal to work and a strike as an effort on the part of misguided men to carry their point by desperate or reckless acts. This distinction once clearly established both as a fact in the conduct of strikes and as a conception of the legal mind, the way was open for those decisions which have declared strikes lawful.

In making a distinction between legal and moral obligations the courts have been generally consistent. The former obligations are such as have already received the sanction of the entire community, and it is the unquestioned province of the courts to enforce them. They are a part of the law. The latter have not such a sanction. They consist of those obligations that are gradually coming to be recognized as having a binding force between various members and between various classes of the community. They are growing out of a constantly changing set of social conditions; they are based on customs that have not yet the sanction of age; and, moreover, they are not recognized universally as binding. For the courts to interfere where such questions are involved would be an intrusion into a sphere where their activity is not permissible. To give the courts jurisdiction over such questions would be to extend their power much beyond their right province of applying to all members of the community such moral precepts and ideals as have been so far accepted by the community as to receive legal sanction. Not until still further progress has been made in the field of social and moral obligations along the line of clearing up and definitely formulating results can these important principles be turned over to the courts for application. It is to be hoped that with the wider recognition of the existence of this class of obligations and the more general agreement as to their morally binding force, many of the difficulties that are now referred to the courts may be settled by other methods. Certainly much is already being done along this line. Both parties are beginning to realize that each can keep within the law and yet adjust differences by amicable agreement. The success of the efforts of the National Civic Federation is proof of this growing opinion. Its realization is also attested by the existence of several local and temporary organizations which in a less public way are accomplishing much in bringing about a wider recognition of moral obligations.

So long as the courts adhere to the distinction between that which is morally right and that which is lawful and insist on basing their decisions on strictly legal considerations, it is difficult to see how they can change their attitude toward the question of motives. The tendency has been to give first a more favorable interpretation of motives, and finally to decline to consider them at all. This is obviously a change in the point of view of the court. It is not at all likely that the motives themselves which prompt a strike have changed materially. Yet in earlier cases the court held them to be primarily to injure others. In later cases they were held to be primarily to benefit the strikers. As a matter of fact, the motive of strikes—if any one motive or any dominant motive at all can be formulated—has always been and still is the desire to improve the strikers' condition, to do so in spite of the fact that others may suffer, and to injure those who are responsible for the unsatisfactory conditions to such an extent that they will yield the point in controversy. When brought face to face with the necessity of deciding a particular case, the courts have succeeded in choosing that line of argument which would best reflect the opinion of the time. When strikes were considered as almost the equivalent of anarchy, the courts were bound to use their influence to prevent them. As public opinion has changed the courts have been able to see more clearly that there were extenuating circumstances. The most recent cases have held that the nature of the motive prompting the act has no bearing on its legality. This development is quite in line with the general tendency of individual liberty which holds one responsible only for his acts. Since in the most recent case the chief justice of the court of appeals has registered his approval of the decision in the leading case in which motives were expressly declared to be immaterial, it is likely that the courts will continue in this opinion.

Economic principles and their application to labor problems have not received much attention. It is of course obvious that it is not the duty of the courts to interpret economic principles. A recognition of such principles and an intelligent application of them is nevertheless to be expected. At this point the courts cannot be accused of entire neglect. Even more than this may be said, for it must be recognized that the primary duty of a court is to interpret the law and apply it to a particular case. To do this successfully a profound understanding of the principles of the law is essential as the first requirement. As a second requirement an understanding of economic and social principles is necessary, for if law is to be what it should be, it must consist in an authoritative statement of such principles in a manner convenient of application.

One of the questions of economics that has received most attention is the application of the law of supply and demand. A reading of the decisions in many cases, especially the earlier ones, gives the impression that the real meaning of these terms was not clearly understood. They were, however, a part of the vocabulary of everyone who assumed to speak of economic principles. In this rather loose way they were used in the decisions. Even while insisting that wages should be fixed by the law of demand and supply, the court seemed oblivious of the fact that both forces must be free to act. Whenever this popular phrase came into contact with the more firmly fixed notion that had grown out of the older industrial relations, the result was usually the declaration, on the one hand, that supply must not be restricted at all, and, on the other, that the employer must not be interfered with in his regulation of demand. Such was the early application of the law of demand and supply. The first important change was made by the enactment that restraint of trade was conspiracy. The decision in the case of People *v.* Fisher interpreted a strike to regulate wages as constituting an interference with trade. In the mind of the justice the conditions of industry were so thoroughly static that to cause trade to pass from one town to an adjoining town was not to be justified in economics. No place was found for dynamic conditions.

When in 1870 the law was secured which gave unions the legal right to endeavor to raise wages, the tendency was not in the direction of the unrestrained action of demand and supply. Custom had for a long time sanctioned the right of the employer to control demand. The law now sanctioned the right of the laborer to control supply. This law the courts interpreted strictly, but even a strict construction admitted the right of laborers to combine for the purpose of controlling wages. Thus, while the free action of demand and supply was being insisted upon as a desideratum, it did not seem to be recognized that the tendency was directly away from such freedom.

The result of the latest decisions has been to give a new direction to the development. One leading case maintained the right to organize and the right to strike if for the purpose of self-benefit. In this way the preservation of competition was secured. If a strike was primarily for the purpose of injuring others, it was interpreted as a stifling of competition. Competition must be maintained. As a matter of fact, organization for the purpose of controlling wages results in the control of supply. Since the employers have always been free to unite, there is in this fact the control of the demand. Both demand and supply can thus be actually regulated. Yet competition, insisted the courts, must be maintained, and further than this there was the implication that this competition must be not potential but actual. In this way the popular cry that demand and supply must be left to work freely was replaced through the actual condition of affairs by the legal dictum that competition must be maintained. The last step has been a logical one. Free actual competition in the field of labor is its own worst enemy. The more free it is the sooner monopoly is established. At this point came the latest court-of-appeals decision declaring that strikes were justifiable, whatever the motive. This had a very important effect. The former case had tried to maintain conditions of competition, and at the same time preserve those conditions from self-destruction. This decision insisted upon free and unrestrained competition regardless of consequences.[1] Labor leaders have expressed their entire satisfaction with this interpretation. If they can organize strongly enough, the way is open for monopoly. Competition may be carried to its logical end, and monopoly may in fact exist so far as legal regulation goes, yet the same law opens the way for potential competition, and potential competition is a powerful check on the evil results of monopoly.

So far as the law goes, then, the way to actual monopoly is open while potential competition is maintained. The same law which makes the one possible makes the other possible also. The struggle is thus transferred to the industrial field, the courts merely insuring the same privileges and the same limitations to all the contestants. The only differences are such as inhere in the nature of the contending parties, and which are, therefore, beyond the control of the law.

While the courts have been developing in the law the application of the principle of individual rights and have been endeavoring to adjust these rights in such a way as to avoid conflict, a new idea has been making itself felt. It is embodied in the question: Are social relations becoming so intricate as to render the exercise of absolute individual liberty impossible? In the days of simple domestic industry, when factories were unknown and when

[1] It is understood, of course, that laws to prevent unlawful means of competition are always in force.

workingmen were in most cases their own employers, individual liberty and social obligation seldom came into conflict. In those days this question never arose. The increasing complexity of all phases of industrial relations has brought the question to the front. It has received many answers. At first the negatives were decidedly in the majority. More recently the affirmatives are growing more numerous.

Absolute individual rights have yielded to reciprocal rights. Reciprocal rights have led to a recognition of the limitations due to association. In theory the source of rights has begun to appear in the group instead of in the individual. At the present time the word "social" has come to have a very large place. Social rights are being urged as the successor to individual rights. This idea is exercising an influence that is very far-reaching. It is urged even as a standard for adjusting industrial disputes. A very important modification is that the number of parties in interest is not limited to two. There is a third party to every industrial controversy—the consuming public.

In laying down the law the courts have spoken very positively of the rights of the employer, and with equal positiveness of the rights of the employee. Few references have been made to the rights of "the third party." One decision that has the approval of the highest court stated specifically that so long as the reason for stopping work seemed good to the striker, it mattered nothing whether that reason seemed justifiable either to the employer or to organized society. Another case has quoted approvingly the statement of Judge Cooley, that "it is a part of every man's civil right" to govern his own acts relative either to work or to trade. The fact that his action may be determined by "whim, caprice, prejudice or malice," has no bearing whatever; "with his reasons, neither the public nor third persons have any concern."[1] *Neither the public nor third persons*, nor in the former case, *organized society*, has any rights whatever in a strike. This attitude is so decidedly at variance with the newer ideas of social rights that it must inevitably be modified sooner or later. Should the cases referred to the courts for decision in the near future increase in number or in importance, this attitude must soon be changed. On the other hand, should the means for settling trade disputes without recourse to strikes be brought to a high degree of perfection, the courts may have no occasion for a long time to alter their decrees.

But to say that this group of rights is being more and more widely recognized is not to say that the courts should immediately adopt it and begin its application. The courts can only act on such principles as are generally accepted and well established. To go beyond this would cause both confusion and discontent. It remains for the courts to wait until the theory of social rights has been more fully developed before using it.

In closing, it remains to point out the fact that moral obligations and social rights are slowly becoming clearer. What use can be made of them in adjusting relations in which labor unions are involved is a question which does not pertain to the legal phases of trade unions. It comes more properly in another study. Judging both from the past records of the courts and the theory on which they are organized, however, it may confidently be predicted that as time goes on these new moral principles will gradually crystallize in judicial decisions, and the labor law will continue to adapt itself, if somewhat tardily, to the ever-changing industrial conditions.

[1] Mills *v*. United States Printing Company.